Led by Examples:

*The Bible's Recipe
for a
Closer Relationship with God*

Led by Examples:
The Bible's Recipe for a Closer Relationship with God
By Donald C. Benson, Jr.

Published by Love, Sharing, Faith Ministry

Copyright © Donald C. Benson, Jr 2017

All rights reserved. No part of this publication may be reproduced, stored in a retrieval system, or transmitted, in any form or by any means, electronic, mechanical, photocopying, recording or otherwise, without the prior permission of the publishers.

The author has made every effort to ensure the accuracy of the information within this book was correct at time of publication.

For requests, information, and more contact Donald C. Benson, Jr at lovesharingfaith@outlook.com

Library of Congress Control Number: 2017918181

Table of Contents

My Testimony 1

Introduction 7

Prayer: How do you talk to God? 17

    Misconceptions about Prayer 17

    Why We Need to Pray 19

        1. To invite God into our lives 19

        2. To engage in fellowship with God 19

        3. Because God told us to 20

    The Prayer Life of Moses 23

    The Prayer Life of David 27

    The Prayer Life of Jesus 33

    Conclusion 44

Praise: How do you show appreciation to God? 45

    The Ways that we Praise 49

    How Moses Praised God 53

    How David Praised God 57

    How Jesus Praised God 63

    Conclusion 65

Perseverance: How do you trust God? 67

The Perseverance of Moses 69

Why We Persevere...75

The Perseverance of David..79

How Jesus Persevered..85

Conclusion...94

Surrender: Can you hand it all over and leave it? 95

How Moses Surrendered 101

How David Surrendered.. 107

How Jesus Surrendered 113

Conclusion... 116

Bringing It All Together.. 117

Great Men and Women of the Bible.. 121

My Testimony

God has been so good to me, but like anyone else, I have had trials and hardships in my life. I am in no way perfect! I was born and raised in a small community in the northeastern part of Virginia. I was the son of middle-class parents. My mom was a stay-at-home mom. My dad was a police officer in Lancaster County, Virginia.

The day that most affected my early life was November 5, 1981. This was the day that my dad was killed in the line of duty. I was a five-year-old little boy who lost his father in the blink of an eye.

I do not have many memories of my dad, but that one tragic event most assuredly reshaped my life. This is not to say that I had a bad childhood; just the opposite is true! My sister and I were raised by one of the best mothers a child could ever want. Our church family at Claybrook Baptist in Weems, Virginia was full of wonderful, caring people. The members of Claybrook treated my mom, my sister, and me with so much love and compassion; it felt like I was everyone's own child. I had a wonderful foundation for my life as a man and as a Christian.

Like many people, as I grew up I questioned everything. I questioned how a loving God could "take" my dad from me. How could a God that my mom served so faithfully have "taken" her husband from her? What had I done at such a young age to be punished like that?

These questions continued to haunt me and linger in my mind as I attended college at Radford University. In the beginning, I looked for a church to join while I was at college, but nothing felt right. So, I thought to myself, I don't need a church. I started to meet new people and made some friends. Little by little, my faith and relationship with God began to wither.

It's funny though; once you become a child of God you can question Him and turn your back on Him, but that doesn't mean He has turned His back on you. He doesn't let you go so easily.

During this time of questioning, my new friends had a big influence on me. I tried to fit in and thought I was having fun. I started drinking, smoking, and doing many other things that I knew were wrong. At this point, everyone around me in my life was doing these things. Eventually, I met a woman that I dated and fell in love with. The potential for disaster lay in the fact that she was an atheist, but at the time I did not think this was a big deal. However, this was the next big thing that changed my life. With all the questions and doubt in my mind, I turned away from God and I married her.

We were young, in love, and life seemed to be good. I was doing anything I wanted. I was trying to make my wife and myself happy. God was totally out of the picture in my life. Deep down, I knew that God loved me and I believed that He was there for me, but I was not worried about God's will for my life; I was worried about my own will. I never thought about prayer or eternal consequences. I was lost.

As we grew older, my wife and I started to grow apart. We reached the point where she told me she didn't love me anymore and asked me to leave. We separated and I moved out of our house. I had nowhere to turn except to a pair of God's angels in my life: my friends Chris and Heather Weeks. These two people loved me, cared for me, listened to me, and advised me. I ended up living on a couch in their basement for over six months. They fed me and gave me everything they could to make sure I was all right.

Even with this tremendous support, I was in a very dark place. I felt like I had lost the love of my life and that I was a burden to my friends and family. I felt worthless and like I had nothing left in my life that could make me happy. I had gotten to the point where I did not want to go on any longer. I was so unhappy.

Then my life changed again. I had been trying to buy happiness for myself and purchased a new smartphone. As most people do, I downloaded a bunch of songs and videos from my computer onto it. One day, I was driving down the road going to work like any other day and decided to hook the new phone up to my car radio. The phone was set on random and the song that came on was one that I had not heard in a long time, and I truly believe it was a direct message from God to me. It was "Jesus Take the Wheel" by Carrie Underwood. As I listened to the first verse, it hit me. I felt something building inside me and I had to pull off the road. Sitting there on the side of the road, it took me about 20 to 30 minutes of just listening as the music moved through me to gather myself. At this point, I started to pray to God for the first time in over 15 years. God sent me that song as a message that day and my life has been changed ever since.

About a week later, I met the true love of my life and my future wife, Heather. She helped me find my way back to the church, and I ultimately turned my life back over to God.

I always felt like I had a calling in life, but fought it for as long as I could remember. In my mind, I tried to do the next best thing—teach. There is nothing wrong with being a teacher;

teachers are some of the best people in the world. Teachers help mold the future, but that was not my definitive calling.

I have embraced my calling of being a minister, evangelist, pastor, and Bible teacher now, and it has led me to this point. I know God has a ministry for me. He led me to start a YouTube channel called "Love, Sharing, Faith" made up of devotionals and sermons that I create with the hope of reaching and inspiring others. Love, Sharing, Faith has expanded to a multimedia ministry that is focused on giving "real talk about real gospel for real life." My ministry is expanding into my evangelistic and pastoral calling with the guidance and inspiration of God.

God has a plan for all of us. This is His plan for me. I want to praise God for the trials in my life as much as the wonderful things He has done for me. God has been there for me even when I was neither working for Him nor wanted anything to do with Him. God is GREAT!

Introduction

It is said that relationships are the centerpiece of human existence. Without good relationships, many people look at life as being less meaningful.

We start building relationships very early in life. These relationships include our relationships with family, friends, and eventually our soul mates. Our desire and quest for meaningful relationships is vital to most (if not all) of the most important aspects of our lives. Most Christians, regardless of how long they have been saved, realize they want and need to have a closer relationship with God. To be honest, who wouldn't want to have a better relationship with God?

As Christians, we want a relationship where we feel like God is our best friend. We are striving for a relationship where we see God as the one we can talk to about anything and everything. God is our Heavenly Father and is there for us. He wants us to be happy and He wants to guide and protect us. It is because of free will that we are sometimes not as close to God as we would like to be.

Our free will is a blessing and a curse at the same time. It gives us the ability to make decisions in our life that can either honor or dishonor God. Like a proud father, when we make the right choices and work to have a closer relationship with God, He looks at us and smiles. However, when we walk away from His side and start to create distance between God's will and our will, I think He tries to guide us back to His side. We see this explained best in Matthew 18:12-14 where it says:

> *How think ye? if a man have an hundred sheep, and one of them be gone astray, doth he not leave the ninety and nine, and goeth into the mountains, and seeketh that which is gone astray? And if so be that he find it, verily I say unto you, he rejoiceth more of that sheep, than of the ninety and nine which went not astray. Even so it is not the will of your Father which is in heaven, that one of these little ones should perish.*

God wants us to have a relationship with Him where we are not just religious, but we develop a bond with Him where we see Him as a partner in life. God wants us to be obedient to His commandments not because He is a dictator with rules we are forced to follow, but because we love Him and want to serve Him.

So, what is the difference between a relationship with God and being religious? Many people think these are one and the same.

Unfortunately, this is the perception that many Christians were taught and grew up believing. These are false teachings and do not represent what God wants. We are not supposed to blindly follow a bunch of rules and then think we are all right with God.

Our relationship with God is personal and unique to each of us. This in no way means that we are not supposed to follow God's commandments, because we are. We are supposed to follow all of His commandments and seek His will constantly. We are supposed to follow the commandments of God because it is our desire to please Him and be of service to Him, not out of a perceived need to obtain something or a feeling of obligation. Granted, if you look at Christians in their day-to-day walk with God, you will see them following God's commandments and striving to avoid sin. This is a byproduct of their relationship with God, not the source.

Why, though, don't we as Christians have the relationship we want with God? Do we think God doesn't want to be close to us? That is nowhere near true. God wants to have a relationship that is so close to us that He is living inside us; a relationship where He guides every step we take and every part of our lives. God tells us in Isaiah 43:2

> *"When thou passest through the waters, I will be with thee; and through the rivers, they shall not overflow thee:*

when thou walkest through the fire, thou shalt not be burned; neither shall the flame kindle upon thee."

If God is willing to walk with us and guide us in these situations, then we should know that He wants to be with us.

With that being said, we have to realize that *we* are the problem. I know it is hard to think about ourselves being the problem in anything, but we must take a step back and be honest with ourselves if we truly want to start experiencing any real spiritual growth.

I like to put it in these terms: God is the constant and we are the variable. God tells us in His word that He is the same yesterday, today, and tomorrow (Hebrews 13:8). If God is not changing, then we are the ones that must change if we want to develop and maintain this closer relationship with God.

If we are looking for the way to a better relationship with God, we have to put in some work. This work can be—and often is—against our instincts, because as humans we have become selfish and self-centered beings. This is the work of the enemy. The enemy to Christians is comprised of a few different things that try to hold us back and hold us down. The main enemy is the devil. We are told in 1 Peter 5:8,

> *"Be sober, be vigilant; because your adversary the devil, as a roaring lion, walketh about, seeking whom he may devour."*

The devil wants to devour us and destroy us.

The next enemy is the world. This is evident in 1 John 2:15-16

> *"Love not the world, neither the things that are in the world. If any man love the world, the love of the Father is not in him. For all that is in the world, the lust of the flesh, and the lust of the eyes, and the pride of life, is not of the Father, but is of the world."*

The world tries to distract us from our calling and from God's voice.

The final enemy we face is our flesh. This is shown in Mark 7:21-23

> *"For from within, out of the heart of men, proceed evil thoughts, adulteries, fornications, murders, Thefts, covetousness, wickedness, deceit, lasciviousness, an evil eye, blasphemy, pride, foolishness: All these evil things come from within, and defile the man."*

The temptations of evil are a tendency of your inward self. Even after you decide to accept Jesus as your Lord and Savior, sometimes your old, sinful cravings will return. You become startled and wonder where they come from. The Bible teaches that the old nature, with all its corruption, is still there and that these evil temptations come from nowhere else.

It has become commonplace to want what we think is best for us and not worry about the true best interests of others. We must work through this, and when we begin to see through the enemy's schemes, we have taken one of the first steps toward developing a deeper relationship with God. However, anything that is worth having will take some work and dedication. You know what they say: "If it was easy, everyone would do it."

The good news is that God is there for us and will reach down as far as we let Him, but there are things we need to do in return. This is what inspired the title of this book.

So where did my idea come from? To start, it came from my personal search for a better relationship with God. Once I began reading the Bible, God led me to several parts, verses, and stories that confirmed the inspiration that He was revealing to me. The key to this confirmation and inspiration was what many people call the "Hall of Faith" which can be found in Hebrews 11 and speaks of some of the greatest men and women of faith in the Bible.

Each verse in this chapter builds on top of the previous one by giving examples of how these great men and women showed amazing faith, and in some cases, courage. As I read over these passages, God laid it on my heart to look at these examples use them as models. So, I looked at their lives and God blessed me with this message and these thoughts. The men and women mentioned in this Hall of Faith had many similarities in how their lives played out.

I looked at how these remarkable people of faith compared to the greatest person we have ever known. I also searched out what we were taught about how to have a relationship with God by His living example. This truly remarkable person, of course, is God's son: Jesus Christ.

After looking at these similarities, I thought and prayed. God guided me to the conclusion that there is a recipe for being closer to Him. Through God's grace and inspiration, He led me to the concept that there are four major things a person must do to have a better and stronger relationship with Him.

Now why do I call the information in this book a recipe for a closer relationship with God? The answer is both simple and complicated. The simple reason is that in any recipe there are variations and individual touches to the way we use it, just as our relationship with God should be created using our unique circumstances and personal influences. The Bible tells us in Philippians 2:12,

"Wherefore, my beloved, as ye have always obeyed, not as in my presence only, but now much more in my absence, work out your own salvation with fear and trembling."

Our personal relationship with God should be just that—individualized.

However, as with any recipe, there are foundational ingredients that you must use in order to make the dish what it is supposed to be. In this case, we must make our relationship with God what He has intended it to be. God told us in the Bible that He knew us before we were even created in the womb (Jeremiah 1:5). He tells us that we are so valuable that He knows the number of hairs on our head (Luke 12:7). With Him valuing us and our lives so highly, is it any surprise that He has a plan for us? He tells us in Jeremiah 29:11,

"For I know the thoughts that I think toward you, saith the LORD, *thoughts of peace, and not of evil, to give you an expected end."*

Do not let the enemy try to trick you into thinking that you are not valuable and that God does not love you. God has a plan for you. It is your job to seek that plan. It will take effort, but it is worth it.

We must use the four main ingredients that will be discussed in this book, but then also add spice and seasonings. In other words, we have to personalize the rest of our relationship with God to *His* individual taste that He has for us. We must remember that the Bible says God knows us intimately. Our Heavenly Father is a loving, generous, and merciful God who allows us to make choices even as He knows we are sometimes making the wrong choice. If we do not seek His will and accept His loving hand in guidance, He will let our free will reign. To step outside of His will for our lives—to try and control all things ourselves—puts us on a path of destruction. That path leads to worry, stress, and loss of peace.

Seek His face—seek His guidance—and you will grow and mature as a Christian. 2 Peter 3:18 says,

> *"But grow in grace, and in the knowledge of our Lord and Saviour Jesus Christ. To him be glory both now and for ever. Amen."*

Grace is a blessing from God that we don't deserve and can't earn. By utilizing the recipe in this book, you will learn how to become more like Christ and grow in grace. By striving to walk daily with Him and pattern your life after His, in His image, the outcome of the recipe will be a very delicious aroma before God.

This is the recipe for a closer relationship with God. The remainder of this book will go into each of the ingredients that we need to focus on, and how the greats of the Bible displayed these characteristics.

Studying the actions and lives of the great men and women of God in the Bible is a wonderful way to learn how we are supposed to build our relationship with God. It really comes down to a simple fact. God wants you, along with all your imperfections, all your shortcomings, all your mistakes; but how much do you want Him? That is a question you need to answer before you get started on this journey of growing closer to God.

This journey will not be comfortable all the time, and it will require daily effort. However, the potential is so great that everything we must do and the changes we must make to achieve our heavenly goal will be worth it. This is the difficult part of the recipe: staying the course to achieve the goal of getting closer to God.

PRAYER:
How do you talk to God?

Prayer is a vital part of our Christian life. However, there are some who say that we don't really need to pray. They argue that prayer is a waste of time. Why would we need to pray if God is omnipotent and knows everything? They argue that if He already has a plan for everything and only plans things in a way that is going to be the best for us, why is prayer needed?

MISCONCEPTIONS ABOUT PRAYER

The truth is that God does have a plan for us and that His plan is in the best interest of His people. However, there are a few major misconceptions about prayer that we need to start with in this chapter.

The first misconception is that we as Christians need to pray to inform God of things in our life or the lives of others. To most people, this makes no sense. God knows all things, so there is nothing we can tell Him that He does not already know. While this is essentially true, God still wants to know all about our lives, including our words, feelings, and actions, and He wants to hear from us in prayer as our acknowledgement of our use of free will. Some of our time spent in prayer should also be spent in reconciliation of our sins that stand between us and God.

Secondly, we do not pray to try to impress God. He does not want or need sweet, poetic words to make Him feel like we are worthy. It has been my experience that we often try to use big words or poetic phrases in prayer, especially when praying out loud in church or amid a group of fellow believers. It is almost as if we want to impress others with our words. This type of prayer is not for God. That is not the point of true prayer. Prayer is intended to be many things, but none of them include getting others to view us favorably or lifting ourselves up.

WHY WE NEED TO PRAY

1. TO INVITE GOD INTO OUR LIVES

Prayer is intended to be a way for Christians to invite God into our lives. This is one of the most wonderful things we can do for ourselves—to ask God to be a part of our lives, help us, and lead us. We take this for granted sometimes. God is gracious and loving. He wants us to willingly come to Him. He will not force himself on us and will not bang down the door to our hearts; we must open it willingly. Initiating prayer is part of us willingly opening our hearts to invite Him inside.

2. TO ENGAGE IN FELLOWSHIP WITH GOD

This is not something we really think about a lot as Christians. However, when we pray as we should, we are almost forming a partnership with God. When we pray, God gives us the joy and privilege of taking part in administrating His kingdom; His affairs. We start working together with Him. The hard, honest truth is that God could do it without us, but we could never do it without Him. What a glorious thing that God allows us the privilege of doing it with Him!

God's plan for us is a definite plan with several specifics involved, but it is also a fluid plan. This means that by praying, we can be a part of creating the ultimate plan for our lives!

3. BECAUSE GOD TOLD US TO

The third reason for prayer is the simplest of them all: God told us to pray. The verse that really showed this to me the most is 1 Thessalonians 5:17-18,

> *"Pray without ceasing. In every thing give thanks: for this is the will of God in Christ Jesus concerning you."*

How can we think we are doing what we are supposed to for God if we do not do this simple thing that He has commanded us? If we expect God to take care of us with the big things in our lives, then we need to be faithful in the small things He commands us to do. Prayer is a part of this. Prayer does not change God; prayer changes us.

Before we go any further, we need to realize that prayer involves active communication. Communication takes two people or parties. Our prayer life is not just us talking to God. It is not just telling Him our needs or wants over and over again. Prayer is also about taking time to listen to God and to wait for the answers to our questions, our requests, and our petitions. Prayer is communication, and communication has to be a two-way activity. If we just talk to God in our prayer lives, we are doing nothing more than lecturing.

Prayer is supposed to be like a telephone conversation, not a telegram. Some of you may not remember the telegram, but we all know how a telephone works. The telegram was a written message transmitted using an electric device. The message was carried along wires, and the text written or printed and delivered to the intended person. Telegrams were commonly used because private telephones were not widespread.

This was a great way to get a message to someone during the 19th and early 20th century. The problem was that the message was sent, but then you had to wait a long time to see if there was a reply. Many times, people would even question if the message ever got to the other party. This is not how our prayer life should be.

Prayer should be like a telephone conversation where we call God up and know that He is there, available to hear us. If we talk to Him, He can and will talk back and will do so immediately if needed. This is not to say that God always replies right away, but He can. We need to be available and listen for this reply.

I know that I need to hear from God on a regular basis. Once I realized that my prayer life was a time of me lecturing to God and not really communicating with Him, my prayer life started to change. I started to give my petitions and requests to God in prayer, and rather than continuing to talk, I would stop and listen for God's answer. I started to seek true communication with God.

The power of prayer is shown in the lives of the great men and women of faith throughout the Bible. To start with, we will look at Moses.

THE PRAYER LIFE OF MOSES

Moses is remembered as a great man of faith, but he was not always that way. He met God and then gained one of the best relationships with God that we know of, in part through his prayers. An example of this is shown in Exodus 17:2-6:

> *Wherefore the people did chide with Moses, and said, Give us water that we may drink. And Moses said unto them, Why chide ye with me? wherefore do ye tempt the Lord? And the people thirsted there for water; and the people murmured against Moses, and said, Wherefore is this that thou hast brought us up out of Egypt, to kill us and our children and our cattle with thirst? And Moses cried unto the Lord, saying, What shall I do unto this people? they be almost ready to stone me. And the Lord said unto Moses, Go on before the people, and take with thee of the elders of Israel; and thy rod, wherewith thou smotest the river, take in thine hand, and go. Behold, I will stand before thee there upon the rock in Horeb; and thou shalt smite the rock, and there shall come water out of it, that the people may drink. And Moses did so in the sight of the elders of Israel.*

This is just one of the many times that Moses prayed to God for help in leading His people. Moses could have been like many of us. He could have tried to fix the problems of the

Hebrew people in the wilderness on his own, but instead Moses went to God for the answers, praying for strength and knowledge to address their situation.

Think about how easy it would have been for Moses to turn his back on the people. Think about how hard it was to listen to the people complaining for 40 years about everything! But Moses was faithful to them and to God.

In fact, one of Moses' most powerful prayers is found in Exodus 33:12-13.:

> *And Moses said unto the Lord, See, thou sayest unto me, Bring up this people: and thou has not let me know whom thou wilt send with me. Yet thou hast said, I know thee by name, and thou hast also found grace in my sight. Now therefore, I pray thee, if I have found grace in the sight, shew me now thy way, that I may know thee, that I may find grace in thy sight: and consider that this nation is thy people.*

This prayer follows quickly upon the building of the golden calf by the people of God when Moses when up to the mount to receive the Ten Commandments. Even Aaron participated with the people of God in indulging in the building of the golden calf (Exodus 32:2). As you recall, Aaron was the brother of Moses.

And so Moses, in his prayer, shows his reflection of betrayal in that he prays, *"Whom thou wilt send with me"* (Exodus 33:12). Perhaps we can speculate at this point what Moses was feeling. Maybe Moses was feeling despair, betrayal, lost, lonely, or discouraged. Or perhaps not, but in any case he cries out to God to be shown the way and to know God.

Moses also entreats God for His great grace in dealing and providing leadership to God's people. The beauty and power of a desperate prayer born from a sincere heart is that God answers. God responded by saying,

> *"My presence shall go with thee, and I will give thee rest"*
> (Exodus 33:14).

In essence, God was saying to Moses that He would go with him. He would yoke Himself with Moses and together they would accomplish the will of God. We are reminded of the same promise of Christ to the believer in Matthew 11:29. The spiritual rest we need to accomplish the work of the Lord is found by understanding and accepting the presence of God in our lives through the presence of the Holy Spirit.

Moses' prayer in Exodus 33 is a prime example of the incredible blessing that is ours today: to commune with God through prayer. His prayer was not flowery, it was not religious, nor was it for show. Moses was candid. It is also important to note that prayer is not a monologue. Prayer is a dialogue with the Infinite Creator.

Indeed God answered, and His response, as is often the case, was a deeper revelation of Himself. In essence, God was saying and affirming again to Moses that He would be with him.; that His presence in Moses' life would be his support, strength, protection, and the grace he needed. In the New Testament, this same commitment from the Savior is captured when He said, *"I am the way, the truth and the life:"* (John 14:6).

To be clear, Moses was not perfect. Moses had times where he slipped and fell away from his faith in God. At one point, Moses paid a high price for not following God's instructions in his life (Numbers 20:12). Even so, Moses is a great example for the leaders of the present and future to look at to learn how to seek God's face and His will. Moses did this through prayer on a regular and continual basis, as we should do today.

Now that we have touched on Moses, who are some other extraordinary people of the Bible that experienced strength and joy through the prayerful lives they led? The Bible has many such examples of exceptional men and women who walked and talked with God.

The next person from the Bible for Christians to use as an example for a rich and full prayer life is David.

The Prayer Life of David

David was called a man after God's heart (1 Samuel 13:14), so he must have been a great example of the way a Christian should live. Like Moses, David was not a perfect person, but he was a blessed and mighty man of God. We need to think about David for a minute as a person before we analyze his great prayer life.

David is a wonderful example for us all because his life spans a whole gamut of conditions. Some remember David as a shepherd boy, others remember him as a warrior, and then others remember him as a king.

David is one of the greatest biblical examples of a faithful servant who ever lived. He was a descendant of Abraham, Israel, and Judah. He was a great warrior, builder, and king. He was the first of his dynasty, which was chosen by God to bring forth His own Son, Jesus.

David was a prophet, poet, and musician. He prayed frequently and fervently. He wrote down many of his prayers and put them to music. A number of these are in the book of Psalms, which has been the prayer book of Israel and the Church for 3,000 years. We can learn some lessons about prayer from David, who certainly knew how to pray. What better person is there to look to for an example of a close relationship with God?

God chooses the lowly and the outcast—those who feel they're nothing in themselves—to raise up as humble instruments to demonstrate His power and strength. David was the youngest son in Jesse's household. He was a shepherd boy out in the field with the sheep. It was a lowly job that meant many lonely hours; hours alone during which he conversed with his Heavenly Father, getting to know Him, His voice, and of hidden preparations for the things to come.

Little David didn't know the great plans God had for him, plans to give him hope and a future. Later in his life, he would often be in very difficult situations, with enemies all around, whether physical or spiritual. When David cried out to the Lord, he knew he could trust Him. David prayed, and he prayed continually.

This is just one of the many prayers that David wrote:

> *"But thou, O Lord, art a shield for me; my glory, and the lifter up of mine head. I cried unto the Lord with my voice, and he heard me out of his holy hill. Selah"* (Psalm 3:3-4).

When David wrote this psalm, he was surrounded and being taunted by his enemies. But what did David do? He trusted God and prayed to Him. This prayer shows the trust David had in God and His protection and might. We can learn a lot from these verses if we just pay attention.

David prayed for protection, favor, guidance, mercy, and help from persecution. That was just within the first seven chapters of Psalms. David knew that God was listening and knew without a shadow of a doubt that God was there for him.

It is said that there are two realities in life: death and taxes. Of course, for the believer there is the all-important reality of the existence of God and His great plan of salvation. Consequently, it may be worth glancing at the last prayer of David prior to his death. That prayer is found in 1 Chronicles 29:10-19.

As an aside, it is important to note that David, as he stands to pray, expresses his disappointment that he was not selected to oversee the building of the temple of God.

However, despite that honest expression from his heart, he begins this prayer by acknowledging that to God and God alone belong greatness, power, glory, victory, and majesty. And so his last recorded prayer begins with praise and thanksgiving.

Additionally, David declares the omnipotence of God by saying that everything belongs to Him and nothing is received by God's creation without God's mercy.

David then praises God and thanks Him. In this public prayer, although a sincere prayer from his very being, David thanks God for His great grace. A grace extended to those who say, as found in Psalm 8:4, *"What is man, that thou art mindful of him?"*

Furthermore, David acknowledges the holiness of God and that those who are called to His heart are called to be holy as He is holy. This call to holiness is affirmed as David states,

> *"As for me, in the uprightness of mine heart I have willingly offered all these things"* (1 Chronicles 29:17).

David is still the leader of God's people and is thrilled and full of joy to see that those present during this prayer are also committed to wholly serving the Lord.

In closing, David prays for others. True servants of God not only pray for themselves, but pray for others as well. The essence of that prayer for others is that their hearts will be totally one with the heart of God. David's prayer also includes a prayer for Solomon, his son and heir to the throne. He does not pray that Solomon will be rich, powerful, or famous. He prays that his son, the soon-to-be leader of the nation of Israel, will have a perfect heart: That perfect heart being defined as one that keeps God's commandments, testimonies, and laws.

How beautiful is the experience of praying for children, especially those children of one's own household? In this world of tribulation that progressively rebels against the grace of God, our children need Christian role models. These role models should not only exemplify Christ in their lives and actions, but should bathe children in prayer to keep them from the evil influences of this world. Ultimately, it is the role of the parent to pray for their children's salvation and for them to have a "perfect heart" towards the Lord.

David realized something that Christians all too often overlook in prayer. Prayer is simply talking to God, whether in a private or public setting. Prayer is communication with God about your thoughts, feelings, desires, and fears. David realized that he needed to talk to God like he would talk to anyone else; not in fancy and pretty words, but just like talking to a best friend. David got it.

THE PRAYER LIFE OF JESUS

I believe that while Moses and David are great examples of Christian life and the way a prayer life should be, the best example for us all to look at would have to be Jesus Himself.

You may be wondering, "Wait a minute, Jesus had prayer in His life? Why would Jesus need to pray to God? He is God." I understand your questions. After all, Jesus is the Son of God. Surely, He didn't have to maintain a great prayer life. This, however, is not the case.

Jesus did not have to pray to communicate with God in the same way that we do, but He did pray. This could have been for any or all of the reasons discussed earlier in this chapter. However, I believe it was based on at least three specific reasons.

First, Jesus prayed to set an example for His followers. This is an example we continue to learn from even as modern-day Christians. Jesus wanted His followers to know how to pray and talk to their Heavenly Father once He was no longer on Earth with them.

Second, the incarnation consists of both divine and human natures. Given His human nature, it was perfectly natural for a Jewish believer such as Christ to pray.

To make this a little clearer, the word incarnation means "the act of being made flesh." It comes from the Latin version of John 1:14, which in English reads, "And the Word was made flesh, and dwelt among us, (and we beheld his glory, the glory as of the only begotten of the Father,) full of grace and truth."

The Bible shows that Jesus was human in many ways. The Gospels report Jesus' human needs included sleep (Luke 8:23), food (Matthew 4:2; 21:18), and physical protection (Matthew 2:13-15; John 10:39). The Bible even shows that He perspired (Luke 22:43-44) and bled (John 19:34). Jesus was human in that He also expressed emotions such as joy (John 15:11), sorrow (Matthew 26:37), and anger (Mark 3:5). During His life, Jesus Himself referred to Himself as a man (John 8:40).

Third, the nature of the Trinity allows for communication between its members. As Jesus was God's beloved Son, He could pray to God the Father.

The Bible shows very clearly that there is only one God, and yet that there are three separate and distinct natures within God. These three distinct natures of God—traditionally referred to as "the Trinity"—are God the Father, God the Son, and God the Holy Spirit.

Each of these three natures of God is distinct from the others but never acts independently. They are one in their nature and purpose. Though the actual term "trinity" is not directly stated in the Bible, it is clear that this philosophy is implied. Some examples of scriptures that demonstrate this are Matthew 28:19; John 10:30, 14:26; 2 Corinthians 13:14.

The thing is, we as humans have finite minds that are not capable of understanding the mystery of God. This fact does not make these facts about God any less true. We have to accept the truths found in the Word of God by faith even though we ourselves cannot understand them fully. For more about this we can look to Hebrews 11:1-6 and 1 Corinthians 2:5-14, 13:12.

This unique relationship as the Son part of the Trinity gave Jesus a little bit of a different perspective than we can possibly have. However, this difference did not mean He had a different prayer life than we are supposed to have. Jesus had direct communication with God—just as we do now due to His sacrifice on the cross. The tearing of the veil at Jesus' death represented this change (Matthew 27:51).

The veil was the separation in the tabernacle between the Holy Place and the Most Holy Place. The tearing of the veil symbolized the destruction of the perceived separation between God and sinful man. Jesus knew what His purpose was on Earth. He would show that there was no true veil that could separate us from God.

Jesus knew that His disciples and future believers were going to need to see and hear Him praying to show that it was and still is a necessary part of life. Prayer was a tool Jesus used for talking to His Father. It is no different for us. Prayer is a direct and meaningful form of communication with our Heavenly Father.

Prayer is the only thing documented in the Bible that the disciples specifically asked Jesus to teach them. They must have realized its importance. To take it even further, Jesus not only taught the disciples how to pray by giving us the Lord's Prayer (See Matthew 6:9-13), but He also showed them the importance of prayer through its results.

Jesus was not just a "do as I say and not as I do" type of leader. As a Jewish man, Jesus knew that prayer to God was a requirement. Jesus was both God and human at the same time. This could make for a tricky balance, but as we would expect, Jesus handled this balance perfectly. So, having been in human form, He was as all of us. Jesus knew of and experienced temptations. Jesus took part in spiritual warfare just as we do today. Jesus prayed early in the morning and, at various points in His life, even prayed all night.

The Bible tells us that near the end of His life, Jesus prayed so intensely that He actually sweated drops of blood (Luke 22:44). There were many documented times in the Bible where Jesus went to a quiet place to pray. I do not see many of us praying so intensely that we start to sweat blood, but the example of this type of prayer life is very clear. Jesus prayed for others and with others. He prayed in public and in private. Jesus prayed before multitudes and in His quiet place. Jesus was a marathon prayer, but He could also be a sprinter. What I mean by this is that Jesus prayed long prayers and short prayers.

Jesus—the Word made flesh—knew the value and importance of fellowship with God His Father through prayer. Consequently, as seen in Luke 6:12, we read,

> *"And it came to pass in those days, that he went out into a mountain to pray, and continued all night in prayer to God."*

Not only does Jesus, by example, teach us the importance of dedicated prayer and waiting for answers, but also the value of solitary prayer and being with God alone.

Furthermore, prayer was so important to Jesus that He gave us a template for how to pray when His disciples asked Him, *"Lord, teach us to pray."* (Luke 11:1). This prayer given to us by the Teacher can be easily memorized and utilized as a prayer to focus our thoughts and hearts upon our Heavenly Father. However, it's also important to remember that fellowship with God the Father is sweet and empowering, and therefore we should set aside periods of time in fellowship and meditation with Him.

It's also important to remember that through the example of our Lord, our prayers should be conducted on a regular basis. The call to frequent prayers is underscored in Luke 5:16, which informs us "*he withdrew himself into the wilderness, and prayed.*" In other translations of this verse the word "often" is included, and here in the King James Version it is implied. In any case, the frequency of the prayers of Jesus is recorded for us throughout the Gospels. Simply stated, the life of Jesus was a constant prayer unto the Lord and is underscored for us in 1 Thessalonians 5:17 which says, "*Pray without ceasing.*"

Probably the most compelling prayer recorded for us in the Scriptures is the prayer Jesus not only spoke but also struggled with in the garden of Gethsemane. The Scripture narrative records in Matthew 26:36-46 for us that Jesus and His disciples went into the garden and Jesus said unto the disciples stay here and I'm going to go on further and pray. However he took the two sons of Zebedee and Peter with him. It is reflected for us in the Scripture that Jesus said unto his disciples that His soul was exceeding sorrowful even unto death. It is also recorded for us that Jesus sweat as it were great drops of blood as he prayed regarding the will of God for Him draped in the shadow of the cross of Calvary.

The importance of prayer is so powerfully exhibited by Jesus in this narrative due to a number of factors. First of all, prayer is not just simply "Lord bless me and God bless others and thank

You." Sometimes we have a misconception of what prayer is. Often we think that prayer is asking God for certain things. This is true as we should pray for one another (James 5:16), offer prayers for healing (James 5:16), pray for our leaders (1 Timothy 2:2), and pray in general (1 Timothy 2:1).

In the garden of Gethsemane, however, prayer is shown to be a struggle. A struggle that depicts the human will versus the will of God. In fact, the struggle for our Lord was so intense that He prayed through His struggle with the will of God three times and then finally resigned His will over to the Father's by saying, "nevertheless not my will, but thine, be done" (Luke 22:42). Consequently, in our own gardens of Gethsemane, we bow our heads and hearts to the will of God and simply express the powerful prayer of *"thy will be done."*

Jesus showed us that even He, as the Son of God, did not expect His prayers to be answered like He wanted all the time. God answers prayer every time. However, sometimes God answers with a solid "No." This can be hard for us. The enemy often tricks us into thinking that these "no" answers are non-answers and that prayer does not work. This is not true. Do not think that God is not listening or that He does not care. God is our Heavenly Father and we mean more to Him than we could ever imagine.

Another thing we need to learn from this example of prayer in the life of Jesus is the importance of praying for God's will. The main obstacle that hinders our prayers is the fact that we are praying for what we want for ourselves and not what God wants for us. We are told in 1 John 5:14-15,

> *"And this is the confidence that we have in him, that, if we ask any thing according to his will, he heareth us: And if we know that he hear us, whatsoever we ask, we know that we have the petitions that we desired of him."*

This passage means that if we are praying for things that are within God's will for us, He has promised to hear us. Unlike humans, God will not lie to us. God's word is His bond and He always holds up His end of His promises. However, this promise is conditional. God has a perfect plan for us, but we have free will. This means that we have choices. These choices affect our lives in more ways than we sometimes realize.

It has often been said that "prayer changes things." But, perhaps most of all, "Prayer changes *me*." In "The Purpose of Prayer," Oswald Chambers states, "To say that prayer changes things is not as close to the truth as saying, Prayer changes me and then I change things."

The Lord's transfiguration, as seen in Luke 9:29, is associated with His praying and the reality that prayer changes me/us. Yes, indeed, when we pray—when we commune with God and enter into His presence—we are transformed inwardly, and others will notice that we have been with the Lord.

God does not like some of the decisions we make in life. We have all made mistakes. These bad choices do not mean He loves us any less, but our sinful choices can sometimes cause Him to stop listening to our prayers. Those sinful choices rooted in rebellion, self-pleasure, and many other types of sin start to conform us to the world and not to God's perfect will.

The example is easier to see when we look at a rebellious child who wants something that needs his parents' approval. Love just radiates out of his heart, as he snuggles on his father's lap preparing to ask the big question. However, this new love plea does not erase yesterday's rebellious actions. His father patiently waits for him to acknowledge his sin, and when he doesn't, the father turns a deaf ear to his son's request. His father longs to bless his son, but knows he can't until he acknowledges his behavior and repents. What hinders our prayers may be a spirit of rebellion!

We have to look ourselves in the mirror and truly work at cleaning up our lives. We need to review any decisions we have made that impact our unanswered prayers. It can be helpful to make a note of conflict areas where we have refused to submit to what God has asked us to undertake. The best way to do this is to ask God to show us where we have detoured from His path.

I understand that sometimes we feel like God is not listening and that we are too far off-track, but that may be because we have strayed too far from His intended path. However, there are a few prayers that God always hears. These are prayers of repentance and prayers for guidance. We need to step up and ask God for guidance to see these things that led us off-track in accordance with His plan. Then we need to confess our rebellion and repent for being distracted by the enemy's plan for our future—repent for making the bad choice which caused us to fall out of alignment with God's plan.

Writing out prayers and possible interpretations of God's will for our lives is one way to develop an action plan to submit our time to His plan. Remember that prayer is communication, and we need to communicate with God to know His plan for us. Taking notes about our prayers and our understanding of God's plan will help us to remember and allow God to correct us if we misunderstand.

I know from personal experience that we all make mistakes and misunderstand God's plan for us. As a young man, I felt a calling for my life from God, but I turned to a teaching career instead of following His true calling on my life to evangelism, biblical teaching, and preaching. After my return to God's grace and accepting God's plan, I wrote down my thoughts on His plan and learned that my written understanding was not exactly what God had intended for me. God wanted more from me than I wanted for myself. God wanted me to continue to teach as I had been doing, but also to move forward in my ministry at the same time. Thankfully, from this misunderstanding on my part came clarity of God's plan for me.

Another time that Jesus Himself prayed is one of the most well-known, well-documented miracles in the Bible and the only miracle documented in all four of the Gospels. Many call it "the feeding of the multitude" or "Jesus feeding the 5,000." No matter what you know it as, most Christians have heard of this miracle. However, many of us forget what Jesus did just before this miracle was performed. He prayed. One account found in Luke 9:16 is as follows:

> *"Then he took the five loaves and the two fishes, and looking up to heaven, he blessed them, and brake, and gave to the disciples to set before the multitude."*

This is an example we all need to follow. Jesus was facing a problem. I am not sure the last time you tried to feed 5,000 men with five loaves and two fish, but I know it would be a problem for me. Jesus, the Son of God, had the power to accomplish this miracle on His own. However, He looked to God before He performed the miracle.

Jesus took the time to look to God in prayer and to seek God's will before moving forward. Jesus knew the importance of giving thanks and the importance of communicating that thanks to God. To reiterate this crucial point, our prayer lives are based on communication and this communication is supposed to be focused on God.

Conclusion

The examples that Moses, David, and Jesus gave us are truly amazing. They all had solid prayer lives, and they all regularly communicated through prayer with God. All three prayed not only for themselves, but for others. The mighty prayers of these men affected many lives. Their examples should still be shining ones to modern Christians. Prayer is a vital ingredient in creating a closer relationship with God. These men show that to be a proven fact.

PRAISE:
How do you show appreciation to God?

In this chapter, we will be looking at the ingredient in the recipe that is possibly the most neglected by Christians: praise. Praise is our way of showing appreciation for what God has done, but it is also a way to show God that we trust Him. Praising God in advance for the miracle we are about to receive shows Him our faith in Him.

God is our Heavenly Father, and we are His children. Many times, we act like spoiled children in God's eyes. God blesses us with so much, and we all too often take it for granted. We almost act as if we expect God to bless us without us showing Him any appreciation or sign of gratitude.

If you have ever dealt with a child that is spoiled, you will understand what I am talking about. The child is given so many things and does very little, if anything, to earn or deserve the gifts they receive. Then this child starts to take these things for granted and does not care for them. The ungrateful child often just tosses them aside, waiting for something else.

Like a parent looking at a spoiled, unappreciative child, God sometimes looks at us when we fail to praise Him in the way we are commanded to, and He decides to put a hold on the blessing that He has for us. Do not misunderstand what I am saying. God does not give blessings to us just to hear or see our thanksgiving and praise, nor does He give us blessings because we really deserve them. We all have fallen short of God's plan and His will for us, but He still loves us and wants what is best for us. However, I believe that the lack of praise will often hinder our future blessings. In Proverbs 11:2 it is said: "When pride cometh, then cometh shame: but with the lowly is wisdom." According to this scripture, pride means trying to put yourself above God, and this pride will interfere with our relationship with and blessings from God

Again, God commands us to praise Him. This may come as a shock or a reawakening. Some may say that God knows our hearts and knows that we love Him, so we do not need to take time to praise Him. Others may think that taking time to praise God in prayer is just for other people or other denominations. I have even heard some groups say that they don't do that in their church because it is disrespectful. The Bible disagrees with that statement.

The Bible states that God commands praise from His people. God tells us in Hebrews 13:15,

> *"By him therefore let us offer the sacrifice of praise to God continually, that is, the fruit of our lips giving thanks to his name."*

This is a commandment, not a suggestion or a request. God commands praise. Now that we have a clear and focused understanding of what God wants and requires of us by our praise, how do we start?

THE WAYS THAT WE PRAISE

Praising God can sometimes be a very personal thing; our praise is individualized. The way you praise God is one of the spices that you use in your recipe for a closer relationship with Him. It will not be and should not be identical for everyone. Your praise is like you: unique.

Some people praise Him with their voice in song; others wave their hands through the air, or run up and down the aisles of the church. Others just lift their hands silently toward Heaven, thanking God. The fact is, no matter what your praise looks like, it needs to be done and it needs to be done regularly. However, all true praise has an aspect of action. In other words, praise is an action word, not a passive phrase.

Praising God might feel uncomfortable at first. I understand this feeling because I came from a church where we did not move or speak during service. The outward expression of praises to God was not something we talked about much, if at all. Learning to be obedient to God and to praise Him was a personal shortcoming of mine for a season of my life. The thing is, our praise life is supposed to be very much like our prayer life: It is personal and it is about communication with God.

We must get past our self-doubt, our self-image, and our herd mentality, because our relationship with God is supposed to be a very personal thing. We are working through our own insecurities to build this line of communication with our Creator. It will be tailor-made just for us. Again, it will be uncomfortable and it will seem almost forced at first, but learning a new thing takes time, patience, and effort.

To be very clear, praise is not only for the church building! We are to praise God continually. This means at work, at school, in the car, at home; anywhere and everywhere we are, we are supposed to be praising God. Our acts of praise may serve as examples to someone else on how to live a Christian life. It may be listening to a Christian radio station or CD in the car on the way to work and just slipping a hand up to indicate to Him that we've heard His message. Whatever it is, it is assured that God hears and sees us.

This is shown in many places throughout the Bible but seems the clearest in

> 1 John 5:14-15: *"And this is the confidence that we have in him, that, if we ask any thing according to his will, he heareth us: And if we know that he hear us, whatsoever we ask, we know that we have the petitions that we desired of him."*

Isn't it great to think that just a small act of gratitude like raising a hand or a "hallelujah" can be pleasing to God? We need to step out of our comfort zone and be willing to humble ourselves before God to show the gratitude we have for Him and His wonderful blessings.

HOW MOSES PRAISED GOD

Moses, being a man of God, understood the value of praise, and he realized that praise is an action word. Moses showed his belief in the value of praise many times in the Bible, and one specific incident is found in Exodus 15:

> *"Then sang Moses and the children of Israel this song unto the Lord, and spake, saying, I will sing unto the Lord, for he hath triumphed gloriously: the horse and his rider hath he thrown into the sea."*

In this recorded example of Moses praising God, we see that it is in response to something wonderful and glorious that God had performed for his people. Specifically, Moses led the Israelites through the parted Red Sea and every Israelite passed through upon dry land. When safely upon dry ground God caused the waters to return and destroy the Egyptian army. Consequently, emanating from the hearts of Moses and God's people was a song of praise.

However, it is important to note that in Exodus 14:31, the Scripture indicates that those who had crossed safely feared the Lord and believed in Him. Therefore, it is important to note that not only did they praise God for what He had done, but praised Him as He revealed Himself in a deeper way. Specifically, Moses and the people praised Him as the Creator of this world as He held back the wall of water. God was praised in that He was and is the strength and salvation of Moses and His people (Exodus 15:2).

It is also important to note that Moses did not turn to the Israelites and invite them in singing a song from the hymnal. Even though formal worship has its place in the church today, it is also central to know that spontaneous praise from the hearts of God's people, in song, can be the most gratifying form of praise offered to God Himself.

One additional spiritual nugget to mine from this example of Moses praising God is that God and God alone is worthy of our praise and should be our focus. As Moses says,

> *"The Lord is my strength and song and he has become my salvation: he is my God" (Exodus 15:2).*

This praise to God continues through verse 21.

In fact in these 21 verses, "God," "the Lord," or pronouns alluding to Him are utilized over 36 times. Therefore, the takeaway for us from the praising of God by Moses in this chapter is that God is truly the only proper object of worship and praise. Not wishing to sermonize, suffice it say that we are not followers of brother so-and-so or this preacher or that teacher. In the words of Paul found in 1 Corinthians 3:5-6,

> *"Who then is Paul, and who is Apollos, but ministers by whom ye believed, even as the Lord gave to every man? I have planted, Apollos watered; but God gave the increase."*

Another prime example of Moses praising God is reflected in the powerful incident recorded for us in Exodus 17:11-13:

> *And it came to pass, when Moses held up his hand, that Israel prevailed: and when he let down his hand, Amalek prevailed. But Moses hands were heavy; and they took a stone, and put it under him, and he sat thereon; and Aaron and Hur stayed up his hands, the one on the one side, and the other on the other side; and his hands were steady until the going down of the sun. And Joshua discomfited Amalek and his people with the edge of the sword.*

This is truly amazing. The power of our praise is overwhelming. Moses did not just stand around and watch the battle that was going on around him; he put his praise life to work. His praise was the key to the victory. Christians need to take this as a literal example. Whether we face trial or temptation, when we are in the middle of a battle with the enemy, we need to praise God. This is because the power of our praise can win any battle.

God does not have favorites. What He does for one person—even a great servant of His like Moses—He will do for any of us. We face battles all the time, and we go through trials and temptations from the enemy continually. The next time this happens to you, think back to Moses and the Israelites in that battle, and throw your hands up to praise God.

That is not the only lesson we should get from this passage and Moses' practice of praising God. People get weary. Our bodies are of this world and are vulnerable to the things that try to wear us down. Moses faced this as well. His arms got heavy and started to fall. This demonstrated that it was not the might of the Israelites that was winning this battle, but God showing His power through the praise of Moses. When Moses' arms went down, the power lessened and the Amalekites began to prevail. When his hands were raised to God, the Israelites prevailed. But Moses was sore, tired, and couldn't continue to keep his arms raised. What did God do? God provided help to Moses in the form of Aaron and Hur.

God sees the struggles we go through and—just as with Moses—He will give to us what we need to be strong and praise Him. With Aaron on one side and Hur on the other, Moses continued to praise. That is what we need to do no matter the situation and no matter the trial. We need to continue to praise God in all of our battles.

How David Praised God

Let's look at David and the example he set with his praise life. David was so full of love for the Lord with an appreciation of the Lord's greatness and goodness, that he said in Psalm 119:164, *"Seven times a day do I praise thee because of thy righteous judgments."*

Seven times a day David praised the Lord. What does this mean? The language suggests that he praised the Lord frequently and habitually with much love in his heart. Considering all God did for David, it is no wonder he praised Him.

David's praise includes petition and confession, but more particularly, thanksgiving and adoration. To praise God means to ascribe glory and worship to Him. David praised God because he saw God as his Heavenly Father. David didn't overlook that his loving Heavenly Father cared for him, watched over him, provided for him, and understood him, just as He does us.

David was a man who was exalted from the lowly position of a shepherd to a warrior and eventually a king. He was anointed king not once, but multiple times and was the ruler over all the Israelites. In 1 Samuel 16:13, David is anointed to become king of Israel, and then after God rejects King Saul (2 Samuel 2:4) David is anointed to be king of Judah, and finally in 2 Samuel

5:3 David was anointed to be accepted as king of Israel by the elders of Israel.

What came first: David's praise or David's anointing? The Bible is very clear that David was worshipping and praising God long before he was chosen to be king, even before he became one of the most famous and mighty warriors in the Bible. Yet all the wonderful blessings God bestowed on David didn't hinder his praise. This is a lesson in and of itself. Many Christians can be blessed so mightily that they start to lack in the praise that should be given to God; this was not the case for David.

An additional lesson about praise we can learn from David is humility. As Christians, we sometimes get off track with our praise and start to sound like we are lifting up our own accomplishments or turning our praise into a pity party.

David was humble in his praise. This is shown in 2 Samuel 7:18:

> *"Then went King David in, and sat before the LORD, and he said, Who am I, O Lord GOD? and what is my house, that thou hast brought me hitherto?"*

David was so humble that even as the king, he knew he had no greater status before the Lord than any other man. David humbled himself before God regularly.

There is a sad "twist" to David's expression of praise in 2 Samuel 12:20. The twist in this narrative is that God's will, probably in David's estimation, was not what he was believing or trusting to happen.

David had sinned, and even though God is merciful and gracious, there are consequences through the laws of both men and God. This sin of David was taking another man's wife—Bathsheba—and then covering up her pregnancy from this illicit relationship by David sending her husband to the front line. As according to plan, Uriah was killed and David thought all would be well. But you can't hide from God.

Consequently, Nathan, a prophet of God, told David his sin was forgiven, but the child that Bathsheba gave birth to would die. However, David prayed for the child's life, hoping God would change His mind. To entreat God for the child's life, David fasted and lay all night on the ground. David entreated God in this way for seven days.

His prayer up to this point was to plead with God for the child's life. His prayer was not only with words, but also in presenting himself in ways that showed him being humble, contrite, serious about his request, and repentant.

Unfortunately, the child died. This outcome was not what David or Bathsheba wanted. Today, we may try to stand in judgment of God and ask why not punish the sinners? Why take an innocent child's life for something done that was not their fault?

The Scripture does not share with us what was on the minds or hearts of David or Bathsheba. In fact there were no questions posed by either of the parents and there was no argument or discouragement towards God.

However, amazingly, we are struck and inspired by the praise of David, the dead child's own father. It is important to note that once David realized that the child was dead, he underwent a physical transformation. He got up from the ground, washed, anointed himself and changed his clothes (2 Samuel 12:20). By taking these physical actions he showed acceptance of the will of God.

It is also important to take note that these actions weren't mere outward tokens of accepting God's will or David just giving "lip service." In fact, in 2 Samuel 12:20, we read that he *"came into the house of the Lord, and worshipped."*

How easy it is to praise God when things are going well and we are living on top of the world. However, in this prayer of David to God to spare the life of his son, we enter into the classroom of accepting God's will. Accepting God's will is the highest form of appreciation for God our Heavenly Father, and in the midst of this appreciation we praise and worship Him despite the circumstances or outcomes.

David was a man of praise and a man of favor. He praised God in word; he praised God in song; and he praised God in music.

David praised aloud with his voice and with his harp. David praised God in all that he did and with all of his heart.

Now that we have looked at Moses and David, let's look again at the perfect example that we were given by God: His son, Jesus.

How Jesus Praised God

As mentioned before, Jesus lived in two worlds at the same time. Jesus was in the spiritual world of His Father—God—and the human world into which He was born. There are not as many documented events in the Bible of Jesus praising God as there were of Moses and David, but without a doubt, Jesus praised God. A particularly clear example of this is found in Matthew 11:25,

> *"At that time Jesus answered and said, I thank thee, O Father, Lord of heaven and earth, because thou hast hid these things from the wise and prudent, and hast revealed them unto babes."*

Jesus knew God was in control. He gave thanks to His Father for His eternal plan.

What we saw in the earlier example was Jesus praising God with His voice in speech. However, this was not the only way He praised. We see Jesus praise God with song as well. When we look at Mark 14:26, we see that Jesus sang to the Lord: *"And when they had sung a hymn, they went out into the mount of Olives."*

Now just to be clear, the events of this time where we see Jesus offering up praise were unique and meaningful. This happened just before Judas betrayed Christ. Jesus knew that He was about to be betrayed and that He was about to face one of the most brutal public executions in history. Yet Jesus chose to praise God with song. That is meaningful.

Jesus was showing us that we are to praise God in all situations and under all circumstances. I know that the times that we have documented occurrences of Jesus praising God are not overwhelming in number, but that does not detract from the fact that the ones we do have are awe-inspiring examples.

I know without a shadow of a doubt that Jesus was a man that praised God, and that He praised Him continually with love in His heart. I do not remember any point in the Bible where it talked about the everyday things of Jesus' or His disciples' lives. The reason I say this is because not all occurrences were recorded and each time Jesus praised God may not have been documented. In fact, most of Jesus' life was not documented. I take this to show that praise was an everyday thing and so common for Jesus that it was not news to the writers of the Bible. That fact in and of itself is a great lesson.

Is our praise so common and done so regularly that it is something that people see as an everyday and ordinary event? This is not to say that we want our praise to be repetitive and meaningless, but think about the things we do every single day. If we were talking to a friend about the day's activities, we would not mention what we had for breakfast or going to the post office or the bank unless something different happened there. We would tell them about the unusual aspects of the day.

In the same way, our praise should become so common that it is not something even mentioned—just expected. This is the way I believe Jesus' praise was. It was so regularly done that not only the people that knew Him and saw Him, but the ones documenting His life in the Gospels did not see it as something that was different and did not mention it.

Conclusion

The examples of praise throughout the Bible are profound. The Bible tells us to offer up the sacrifice of praise continually in Hebrews 13. Many times, we don't see our praise as a sacrifice like the examples in the Bible. The Bible tells in Leviticus about all the sacrifices that the people often were required to voluntarily provide. We live now under the ultimate sacrifice that was given by Jesus on the cross for us. This ultimate sacrifice has given us freedom from the ritualistic sacrifices of old.

This wonderful gift that was given to us with grace and mercy is not an exemption from the sacrifice of praise that we are instructed to give. The sacrifice of praise is a requirement and is vital to a closer relationship with God. If your praise is mighty, your power will be enormous as well and your relationship with God will grow.

PERSEVERANCE:
How do you trust God?

One of the most difficult parts of being a Christian is learning to deal with the fact that becoming a disciple of Christ does not make us immune to life's trials and tribulations. Many times Christians, especially newer ones, will wonder why a good and loving God would allow us to go through awful things in life like the death of a child, disease or injury to ourselves or loved ones, financial hardships, or worry and fear.

The Bible clearly teaches that God loves those who are His children, and He *"works all things together for good"* for us (Romans 8:28). That must mean that the trials and tribulations He allows in our lives are part of the working together of all things for good. Therefore, for the believer, all trials and tribulations must have a divine purpose. There are many examples of perseverance in the Bible. As we have done in the earlier chapters, we will look at the lives of great men of faith in the Bible as examples of how God encourages us to persevere.

THE PERSEVERANCE OF MOSES

Moses was a man who persevered for God's will to be done, in God's time. He persevered despite many hardships and setbacks. His whole life is a story of perseverance. Rather than looking at and quoting the majority of Exodus, Leviticus, Numbers, and Deuteronomy, I believe it will be better to just look at Hebrews 11:23-29:

> *By faith Moses, when he was born, was hid three months of his parents, because they saw he was a proper child; and they were not afraid of the king's commandment. By faith Moses, when he was come to years, refused to be called the son of Pharaoh's daughter; Choosing rather to suffer affliction with the people of God, than to enjoy the pleasures of sin for a season; Esteeming the reproach of Christ greater riches than the treasures in Egypt: for he had respect unto the recompence of the reward. By faith he forsook Egypt, not fearing the wrath of the king: for he endured, as seeing him who is invisible. Through faith he kept the Passover, and the sprinkling of blood, lest he that destroyed the firstborn should touch them. By faith they passed through the Red sea as by dry land: which the Egyptians assaying to do were drowned.*

Moses' life of perseverance in the face of hardship began at his birth. He was born during a time when the Jews were enslaved in Egypt. To make matters worse, the Pharaoh of Egypt had ordered all males born of Hebrew parents to be killed at birth. Pharaoh was attempting to keep the population of Jews from growing.

In an effort to save Moses' life, his mother had his sister put him in a basket and send him floating down the Nile River. It was by God's design that the Pharaoh's daughter heard Moses' cries and had him pulled out of the water. She adopted the child and raised him as an Egyptian prince. To show God's love of Moses even further, God allowed Moses' sister to be watching as the princess pulled him from the water. God softened the princess' heart to the offer made by Moses' sister to go find a nursemaid that could breastfeed the baby until he could be weaned. The sister did this, of course, so she could get Moses' own mother to be this nursemaid. God had shown the way to save Moses and make sure his mother had a hand in raising him in his most formative years (Exodus 2:1-10).

Later in his life, Moses saw an Egyptian overseer beating one of the Hebrew slaves. Something snapped within him. He killed the overseer and in turn, Pharaoh ordered Moses to be killed. This led Moses to run off to Midian where he immediately ended up in a confrontation with some shepherds who were abusing seven women there. Moses married one of the women and became a shepherd of his father-in-law's flock of sheep (Exodus 2:11-3:1).

Isn't it funny how God works? God had a plan for Moses and the steps of his life had been ordered to this point for God's purpose. Moses had no idea what his future would hold or what God had planned for him. God placed Moses in Midian tending sheep with his wife and her family. He maneuvered circumstances and moved Moses into position to prepare him for what was in store.

Eventually, God revealed Himself to Moses in the form of a bush that was on fire, but never burned up. He told Moses that he must go to Egypt and give the Pharaoh God's message: *"Let my people go."* (Exodus 5:1).

Unsuccessfully, Moses tried to get out of God's mission. He used a series of excuses such as saying that he didn't speak well. He stuttered and questioned why anyone would listen to what he would say. God told him to bring along his brother, Aaron, to do all the talking. Moses kept trying to come up with excuses, but God kept coming up with answers.

Finally, Moses agreed to go and deliver God's message to Pharaoh. Of course, the Pharaoh's answer was no. God had this all under control. Even though it was not until God sent ten different plagues upon Egypt, the Pharaoh finally agreed to let the Jews go. However, shortly after he granted them freedom, Pharaoh changed his mind and chased after Moses and the Jews to bring them back (Exodus 14).

The Israelites were eventually caught between the Pharaoh with his army and the sea. This is one of the greatest moments in the Bible. The Israelites were crying and complaining to Moses as the Pharaoh and his army was closing in to take them back into captivity or worse, kill them. Moses had to make a choice. He had to decide whether to persevere and trust God, or to give up and surrender to the Egyptians like his followers wanted him to do. As you know, this is what Moses did according to Exodus 14:13-14:

> *And Moses said unto the people, Fear ye not, stand still, and see the salvation of the* LORD, *which he will shew to you to day: for the Egyptians whom ye have seen to day, ye shall see them again no more for ever. The* LORD *shall fight for you, and ye shall hold your peace.*

Such was the degree of faith that Moses had in order to persevere in the face of danger, chaos, and certain death. None of these fazed Moses. He did what he knew to do: he faced the problem. Moses looked to God knowing that if he waited on God's plan, it would be greater than anything he could have done within himself.

The relationship and trust that Moses had in God allowed him to stand firm, and he was able to look at the obstacles in front of him and continue to trust in God's will.

Perseverance is about trust. We must trust that God has a plan for us and that we are always under His protection and favor. It can be difficult to do, but sometimes we must stand still in order to move forward.

The idea of standing still and waiting for God to work was very hard for me. I grew up in an athletic family. We believed in hard work and practice. I cannot count the number of times I heard the phrase, "If you are not moving forward, you are moving backward." This may be true for many parts of life, but it is not true with our spiritual lives and the spiritual battles we face.

After all of the events described above, Moses led the Israelites through the desert for 40 years. Throughout this entire time, the Israelites constantly kept running to Moses, complaining about the trials they faced and the troubles they were having. Moses knew what to do. He turned to the Lord and persevered. When the Israelites were hungry, God gave them quail. When they complained of no bread, God gave them manna. When they griped about being thirsty, God told Moses to strike his staff against a rock and water burst forth.

During this time in the wilderness, God called Moses up Mount Sinai and gave him the Ten Commandments. Imagine how Moses must have felt to be chosen by God to deliver something so important!

Throughout this whole time wandering the wilderness, the Israelites had to learn to develop their faith in God. They were ungrateful and complained the whole time. As their leader, Moses was always the one they blamed for their misfortune. However, Moses continued to persevere through it all. He kept working toward his goal and never gave up.

WHY WE PERSEVERE

Perseverance is a huge part of being in a real relationship with God. God has a plan for all of us, but it is in God's time and not ours.

God makes us persevere for a few reasons. The first is to teach us appreciation for what we have; what He has blessed us with. Remember earlier when I mentioned the child that is given everything that he or she ever wanted? The child will never really appreciate the things he or she is given.

God wants to bless the people that serve Him. He longs to give us everything we want and need. However, God is our Heavenly Father and treats us the same way as that human father. He does not want to spoil us, and He wants us to appreciate what we have.

God wants us to persevere so that we have a chance to really think about what we are asking for. Look at it like this: How often do you ask for something you think you really want, but then realize when you get it that you didn't actually want it? Perhaps it turned out to be more of a hindrance than it was worth?

God has us persevere so that we can make sure we realize what we are doing. It sounds crazy that a person would ask for something and not really want it, but this is true for us spiritually many times. The reality is that we are human, and we do not need to know God's reasons. When God answers a prayer, He does it His way, and sometimes He wants to give us time to think about what we are asking for so that when it happens, we are ready.

God's plans are always better than our plans. Just as a good father will not let his children get in over their heads with something they are not ready for, God will not give us what we want right away because we may not be prepared to deal with it.

Another reason we need to persevere is because the challenges in our lives make us stronger. They build us for the future. God puts things in our lives to challenge us and prepare us for the great things He has planned for us.

Just as a blacksmith must heat steel to form it, God does the same with us. The fire does many things to the steel. It makes it bendable so that it can be shaped. Also, the heating of the steel will burn off impurities in the materials to make them as pure and strong as possible. This process of heating and shaping and purifying is like what God does for and with us. Psalm 66:10-12 gives a clearer view of the way God uses the things in our lives to help build us:

> *For thou, O God, hast proved us: thou hast tried us, as silver is tried. Thou broughtest us into the net; thou laidst affliction upon our loins. Thou hast caused men to*

> *ride over our heads; we went through fire and through water: but thou broughtest us out into a wealthy place.*

If we as Christians can persevere, then we will be stronger, wiser, and more prepared for the things that will come as part of God's plan for our lives. God knows His plan for us. He knows where we need to be pushed in our lives to gain the strengths and abilities we need.

Another example that shows this idea is a caterpillar in a cocoon. After metamorphosis, the new butterfly must escape its cocoon. This struggle is how the butterfly's wings get strong enough so that it can fly. The worst thing that could happen to a butterfly at this point is if someone were to cut the cocoon open to try to help. This is because the butterfly's wings will never get the opportunity to be strengthened. The wings will be too weak and the butterfly will be crippled by the lack of strength.

We are much like this butterfly. We need the struggles in life to be strong in the future and to fly to the heights to which God wants us to soar.

Finally, God has us persevere because it fits His big picture. We only see a very small part of God's eternal plan. God has the plan laid out for all things to work together for the good of the people that serve and love Him. God's plan does not work on our schedule. It only works when we are willing to persevere until the right time and place come together for the blessings we want.

Even though Moses was a great example of perseverance in the Bible, he was definitely not the only example we find of this essential ingredient for a closer relationship with God. Again, we will take a look at the life of David.

THE PERSEVERANCE OF DAVID

Our first introduction to the Biblical character who will be known as a *"man after God's own heart"* (1 Samuel 13:14) is found in 1 Samuel 13. The prophet Samuel was instructed by God to go to the house of Jesse to anoint the next King of Israel. The rejection of Saul as the King of Israel is due to the fact that Saul was disobedient by not following the instructions and commands of God.

And so, along with Samuel, we enter the house of Jesse (1 Samuel 16:5). Jesse has a total of eight sons and each of the first seven sons pass before Samuel to determine whether the son of Jesse standing before Samuel is to be God's newly anointed king. It is interesting to note that the assumption of Samuel, when looking at the first son by the name of Eliab, was that this would be the man that God had chosen. He based his assumption solely upon his outward appearance for he must have impressive physically. However, God states in 1 Samuel 16:7,

> *"look not on his countenance, or on the height of his stature; because I have refused him: for the Lord seeth not as man seeth; for man look upon the outward appearance, but the Lord look at on the heart."*

And so this is repeated seven times and seven times each son is refused by God. Finally, Samuel asks Jesse if there are any other children and Jesse responds that there remains yet the youngest and he is out in the pasture with the sheep. David, the man after God's own heart, is summoned and stands before Samuel and Samuel is instructed to take the oil and anoint David as God's future king.

In addition to this being a teachable moment for David about perseverance, it is also important to note that even God's prophet was taught about perseverance. This lesson on perseverance to Samuel is due to the fact that he persevered through this anointing process by not anointing the individual that he perceived to be the heir to the throne, but instead selected the Shepherd King, based on David's heart and not physical appearance, to be the next ruler of God's people.

Thus begins David's spiritual education as he is anointed the future King of Israel. Many biblical scholars estimate the age of David at this point to be between the ages of 8 and 15 years old. His perseverance is reflected in the fact that he then didn't ascend to the throne of Israel until the age of 30. Therefore, the promise of God to David to be the next King of Israel spanned anywhere from 15 to 22 years. This certainly is a reflection of the perseverance of David and his belief in the promise of God regarding his being anointed the next king.

With the definition of perseverance being the demonstration of being determined, persistent, or having the tenacity to follow through on achieving a goal or staying the course, we move into another example in David's life of exhibiting perseverance.

The battlefield where David exhibits his persistence is both a spiritual and a physical battlefield. It is the battlefield where he encounters the giant hero of the Philistines known as Goliath.

Each day, on the battlefield between the two warring nations of the Philistines and the Nation of Israel, a warrior by the name of Goliath walked out towards the Israelite army and challenged any of their warriors to a personal conflict. Goliath slandered the name of God in an effort to provoke a willing or unwilling hero from the Israelite army to emerge. He was not successful.

However, one day Jesse sends David with food for his brothers who are engaged in the war. While he is there, Goliath once again goes through his routine. David becomes enraged because Goliath is slandering the name of God. Consequently, David goes to King Saul to ask for permission to engage the Philistine hero.

And so the inspirational story unfolds, and armed only with his shepherd's sling, David aims straight and true and knocks the giant unconscious and then beheads him.

What a wonderful, motivational, and compelling reality for the believer in studying and applying the perseverance of David in this situation. David was called by God and realized the power of God's touch upon his life through the anointing of Samuel. Consequently, David persevered in this situation—through his faith and the reality of his calling—and physically killed the giant Goliath. His perseverance in his faith and calling solidified his anointing and brought glory and honor to God.

As equally important, it is critical for the believer to also realize that they have this same anointing and calling by God that can cause them to persevere by faith in being God's chosen.

Following David's heroic actions against the giant Goliath, the popularity of David grew in leaps and bounds. In fact, the people would say that Saul had killed his thousands and David had killed his ten thousands (1 Samuel 18:7). This enraged King Saul to the point where David started to fear for his life and eventually, through the help of Saul's son Jonathan, he began a life on the run. On two separate occasions, David had the opportunity to kill the reigning king. These narratives are found in 1 Samuel 24:3 and 1 Samuel 26:7-12.

Once again, what a glowing example of David's perseverance as it relates to the timing and the will of God! How easy it would have been to kill the one who was trying to kill him, but David refused because Saul was still God's anointed. It is extremely important to note that David accepted his circumstances, the sovereignty of God, and God's will for his life through his solid faith and perseverance in trusting God. David knew that the One who had promised was faithful and that His promises would come to fruition in His perfect timing. Therefore, it is important for us as believers as well to believe the Word of God and trust in Him despite where we may be in life or what may be happening to us.

Remember we are in warfare as well, but for the Christian our warfare and our wrestling is not physical in nature but spiritual. The reality of the Christian's experience as it relates to warfare is reflected in Ephesians 6:12, which reads,

> *"For we wrestle not against flesh and blood, but against principalities, against powers, against the rulers of the darkness of this world, against spiritual wickedness in high places."* Persevere in the strength of the Lord!

Now that we have looked at Moses and David for examples of perseverance as an ingredient for a closer relationship with God, we need to look to the greatest example once again: Jesus.

How Jesus Persevered

Jesus was sent by His Father to redeem mankind with His own life as the ransom price. He will someday return mankind to the viable relationship with God that was first enjoyed by Adam. Jesus knew that His consecration to God would bring Him many trials and much suffering. His impending sacrificial death was a commitment that He came to fulfill.

During His ministry, Jesus faced adversity from His family, His disciples, the people of Israel, and religious and political officials seeking to entrap Him. Perseverance was essential to maintaining focus on His mission during those challenging times.

Jesus' taught the disciples that perseverance was essential in their own commitment. As He said in Matthew 7:13-14:

> *"Enter ye in at the strait gate: for wide is the gate, and broad is the way, that leadeth to destruction, and many there be which go in thereat: Because strait is the gate, and narrow is the way, which leadeth unto life, and few there be that find it."*

Jesus' teaching on perseverance was vital to the disciples and us because it emphasized the value of not giving up. Jesus teaches that the time when we start to turn back and give up is many times the moment right before God is about to step into the situation on our behalf.

Jesus often taught in parables. In Luke 11:5-10, He told a story of a man who went to his neighbor at midnight, saying that he needed bread for a visitor. His neighbor at first refused to give him anything, but after persistent pleas finally gave in. This illustrates that we should persist in seeking God's blessings:

> *"So I say to you, ask and it shall be given you; seek, and ye shall find; knock, and it shall be opened unto you: For everyone that asketh receiveth; and he that seeketh findeth; and to him that knocketh it shall be opened"* (Matthew 7:7).

In another parable, Jesus taught about the value of persistence in prayer:

> *And he spake a parable unto them to this end, that men ought always to pray, and not to faint; Saying, There was in a city a judge, which feared not God, neither regarded man: And there was a widow in that city; and she came unto him, saying, Avenge me of mine adversary. And he would not for a while: but afterward he said within himself, Though I fear not God, nor regard man; Yet because this widow troubleth me, I will avenge her, lest by her continual coming she weary me. And the Lord*

> *said, Hear what the unjust judge saith. And shall not God avenge his own elect, which cry day and night unto him, though he bear long with them?* (Luke 18:1-7)

Just as the woman in this parable was persistent in her request to the judge, so we need to also be in our prayers. Jesus knew that we are weak and that in the face of trials and tribulation and ridicule we would be prone to lose heart and quit praying. This parable is supposed to be a constant reminder to continue to pray even when the situation seems hopeless.

In Matthew 15:21-28, Jesus healed the daughter of a Gentile woman after her persistence appealed to His compassion. He said that her faith was great. Thus, persistence demonstrates faith. As shown in Matthew 15:28:

> *"Then Jesus answered and said unto her, O woman, great is thy faith: be it unto thee even as thou wilt. And her daughter was made whole from that very hour."*

Perseverance indicates a working faith that we must have to progress toward a closer relationship with God.

However, Jesus did not just talk about perseverance; He lived it. Jesus was not born in a palace like one would expect for the King of kings and Lord of lords. He was born in a stable and placed in a lowly manger. Jesus was not born into a royal family, but into that of a carpenter. In those times, a carpenter was seen as being a lowly position and had little to no honor in its craft. Jesus came to the world in a human form as the lowly son of a man and woman who were not of any great stature in the community.

The Bible does not give much detail about Jesus during His youth, but we know that He worked as a carpenter while a young adult. It is believed that He began His ministry at age 30, when He was baptized by John the Baptist, who recognized Him as the Son of God.

After His baptism, Jesus went into the Judean desert to fast and meditate for 40 days and nights. This alone is a great example of perseverance. Fasting for 40 days and nights is not an easy task. However, this is not the whole story.

During His time of prayer and fasting, Jesus was tempted by Satan three times, as is chronicled in the books of Matthew, Mark, and Luke. As most will recall, the enemy appeared to tempt Jesus: once to turn stone to bread, once to cast Himself off a mountain where angels would save Him, and once to offer Him all the kingdoms of the world over which He could rule. All three times, Jesus rejected the devil's temptation and sent him away. In other words, Jesus persevered.

The Bible does not give much detail about Jesus during His youth; His first words that are recorded for us were when He was 12 years old. When he was separated from His family, after attending the feast, it appears that His family was frantic at being separated from one another. When they found Him at the temple they said they were worried. Jesus' reply is recorded for us in Luke 2:49 when He says, *"How is it that you sought me? wist ye not that I must be about my Father's business."*

Thus we see the discipline and focus of this young boy from the onset in that He was to be about what God required and needed. This focus or perseverance of our Lord Jesus is seen time and time again. God's business was His business.

It is compelling to note that following John the Baptist's declaration regarding the Spirit of God descending upon Jesus as a dove, Jesus was led by the Spirit. Interestingly, though Jesus was led to minister to people, He did not perform miracles right away nor did He begin to preach. The Scriptures record for us that Jesus was led into the wilderness: a place of loneliness, seclusion, barrenness, or desolation. Additionally, as seen in Matthew 4:1, the intent of God was for one reason and one reason only. The business agenda of The Father was for His son to be tempted or tested.

The message of perseverance is very clear for us as believers in that God's agenda for our lives as well is for us to be tested. For some believers, the response may have been, "I didn't sign up for 40 days in the wilderness." But please remember God has an individual plan for each of us and that plan is for us to be tested so that our faith may increase (James 1:2-3). Consequently, if God required this of His Son, then how much more will God's plan for us be a call to perseverance?

Following the leading of Christ into the wilderness, He then attend a wedding in Cana in Galilee as documented in John 2:1-11. This event will be the backdrop for Christ's first miracle: the changing of water into wine, and not just ordinary wine, but a wine so delicious to the taste. Although, it may not appear to be an indicator of the perseverance of Jesus, it demonstrates the response of the Lord to those who persevere in their faith. Specifically, Mary is informed by the Lord, following her statement about there being no wine, that *"mine hour is not yet come"* (John 2:4). However, Mary does not relent, but perseveres. She says to the servants, *"Whatsoever he saith unto you, do it"* (John 2:5). Mary persevered, and her perseverance was honored with the water being turned into wine.

Consequently, it is important for the believer in this instance to understand the role of persevering in faith to please God. At the wedding in Cana, Christ honored the wedding through his mother's perseverance.

As Jesus continued preaching about and demonstrating the arrival of the Kingdom of God, the crowds grew larger and began to proclaim Him as the son of David and as the Messiah. His popularity was increasing. The Pharisees heard of this and publicly challenged Jesus, accusing Him of having the power of Satan. He defended His actions with a parable, then questioned their logic and told them that their narrow-minded thinking denied the power of God, which only hardened their resolve further to work against Him. (Luke 11:14-23)

So again, Jesus persevered. His mission—in accordance with God's plan—was to *"preach good tidings unto the meek."* (Isaiah 61:1) In Luke 4:21 Jesus says, *"This day is the scripture fulfilled in your ears."* Jesus, the Word that became flesh, was called to preach in season and out and He would not be deterred. His perseverance to sow the seeds of the Word should speak volumes to those called to preach in word and deed. Do not give up, do not be deterred by others who speak against you and others, but share the gospel.

Near the city of Caesarea Philippi, another powerful instance of the Lord's perseverance through difficult times is unveiled from those within His inner circle. In Matthew 16:15-23 we have recorded for us an amazing story of confession from Peter on who Christ is and then, almost immediately, a rebuke given to the same Peter.

Jesus asked His disciples a question regarding His identity. After He asked, *"Whom do men say I the Son of man am?"* (Matthew 16:13), various responses were given as to His identity. Then point blank Jesus asked of His disciples, *"But whom say ye that I am?"* (16:15), Peter answered, *"Thou art the Christ, the Son of the living God"* (16:16). But it seems immediately upon this declaration that Jesus, because He is the Christ, reaffirmed His mission within His own heart and mind.

In Matthew 16:21, Jesus confided in His disciples that He had to go to Jerusalem to suffer, be killed, and be raised the third day. He persevered by stating His mission and ministry as *"the Lamb of God that taketh away the sin of the world"* (John 1:29). Then, surprisingly, Peter contests this by stating that it will not happen.

However, Jesus recognizes the influence of this statement emanating from Peter and says, *"Get thee behind me Satan"* (Matthew 16:23). Remember, even well meaning acquaintances or friends in our sphere of ministry or friendships may try to deter the mission or calling that God has for us. It is important to recognize those adverse influences and stay the course. As our Great Example demonstrates His perseverance, so we must persevere as His followers.

One additional example of Christ persevering is in the face of betrayal. At the last supper, Judas Iscariot had already determined in his heart to betray the Lord. Jesus, knowing this, took up the servant's towel and a basin of water and washed the feet of all His disciples including Judas. This action of the Lord is so dynamic in that it not only shows His servant's heart but also His service of love even to those who would betray Him. Remember, it was not only Judas that betrayed Christ, but also Peter, who denied Him three times, and the other disciples, who scattered in fear of their own lives.

Our glorious Lord was basically deserted by everyone. Even God, as Jesus hung from Calvary's tree, caused darkness to fall on the scene, as God could not look on sin. This is evidenced as Christ called out, *"My God, my God why hast thou forsaken me"* (Matthew 27:46). Our Savior was betrayed, mocked, tortured, crucified, and those He called friends deserted Him.

Despite it all, however, Jesus Christ was faithful and obedient. In Philippians 2:8 we read, *"And being found in fashion as a man, he humbled himself, and became obedient unto death, even the death of the cross."* Jesus Christ persevered by faith.

Anyone who could persevere through everything leading up to this point would be labeled a hero of the faith and the story would end, but not for Jesus. His story continues; the Son of God persevered even through death.

Three days after His death, Jesus' tomb was found empty. He had risen from the dead and appeared first to Mary Magdalene and then to His mother. They both informed the disciples, who were in hiding. Later, Jesus appeared to them and told them not to be afraid. During this brief time, He beseeched His disciples to go into the world and preach the gospel to all humanity. (Matthew 28:19)

After 40 days, Jesus led His disciples to the Mount of Olives, east of Jerusalem. Jesus spoke His final words to them, saying that they would receive the power of the Holy Spirit, before He was taken upward on a cloud and ascended into heaven. (Acts 1:9-12)

Jesus and His example would not have been the same without obstacles. He was both human and God at the same time. If He never faced any hardships, there would be no example of His humanity. Jesus showed in His words, His actions, and even in His death and resurrection that we need to persevere.

Conclusion

Perseverance is a vital ingredient in the recipe for a closer relationship with God. Through these examples in the Bible, we can see how truly important it is. These men realized something that we all need to realize: The moment when we most want to give up—the moment life gets the hardest—could be the moment right before we reach the end goal. It is said that the night is darkest right before the dawn. As Christians, we need to remember this. The enemy wants us to give up because he knows it is the only way he can win.

SURRENDER:
Can you hand it all over and leave it?

The final ingredient for a closer relationship with God is probably the most important one, because it makes the other three work together cohesively. God wants us to surrender to Him. Surrender our hearts, surrender our selfishness, and surrender our plans for our lives. Surrendering our hearts, minds, and souls to God is the key to making our lives more meaningful and fulfilling.

The thing that confuses many Christians is that they think they are losing their individuality or themselves in the process of building a close relationship with God. This is so far from the truth. God made us individuals and He made us to be ourselves, but by surrendering ourselves to God we are reaching the full potential that He has for each one of us.

God created each of us for a purpose. God created us to be unique. So why would He want us to change to have a closer relationship with Him? Why would we think that God wants us to be like anyone or anything else? God wants us just as we are, but He wants us to surrender ourselves to His plan and His will for us.

God gives each of us talents as well as unique and special features that He intends for us to use to advance His purpose and will for us. However, we live in a time where we are on a battlefield between the mortal world and God.

This began as early as the Garden of Eden. Since the original disobedience of Adam and Eve, the world we live in has been in conflict. We have a daily choice to make. We must choose to try to fight this battle ourselves, or we can let God be the one that fights for us. I don't know about you, but I like being on the winning team—and the Bible shows us in Revelation 17:14 that God wins the ultimate battle

> *"These shall make war with the Lamb, and the Lamb shall overcome them: for he is Lord of lords, and King of kings: and they that are with him are called, and chosen, and faithful."*

If we already know the outcome of the war, why do we choose the losing side? Honestly, given our free will, we don't always realize what side we are choosing. Satan tries to trick us in many ways. He is a master deceiver. The biggest of these lies is convincing us that we have already asked for help and God doesn't care enough to help. Instead of waiting for Him to fix things in His perfect time, we try to run ahead of Him and put our own solution in place. We claim to seek God for an answer to a problem or something else we want, but then we try to fix it in the way we think is best.

I know for years I thought I was doing the right thing. I thought I was going through life in a Christian way. The truth was that I was trying to fight all the battles in my life myself. The things that I thought I had turned over to God, I really had just gone to God with. Then when I was done telling him the things I needed or wanted, I would pick those things up again and try to fix them myself.

Surrendering our lives to God essentially gives us the clarity to work with Him and allows Him to guide our path with His battle plan. As it says in Psalm 37:23, *"The steps of a good man are ordered by the Lord: and he delighteth in his way."* Since God knows all, sees all, and His thoughts are higher than our thoughts, why would we not want to look to Him for our futures?

We need to realize that surrender to God cannot be a conditional surrender. God does not make treaties, and He does not negotiate. We cannot expect to have a closer relationship with God while still trying to hang onto things in our lives. We cannot come to God and say, "Lord, I give this over to You, but only if I can still do it." That simply will not work. Also, we sometimes come to God and try to say, "Okay, I will give this to You, but only if You do this my way." That will not work either.

God is not going to bargain with us, and He will not accept our conditional terms. He wants our whole heart, our whole mind, and our whole spirit. He loves us so much that He does not want to give us just part of His blessings. He wants us to have the whole thing. However, if we are not willing to surrender our lives to Him, He cannot give us our full portion of blessings.

What does a surrendered life look like? Surrendering to God is not exactly giving up total control over every single little thing. Obviously, we still need to make choices about our daily lives and plan for the future.

Surrendering to God is more about aligning what you want with what God wants and being willing to follow Him as He guides you in your life. Surrendering your life to God is choosing to allow Him to take the lead on what happens.

Yes, work hard at your job. Yes, take the time to speak in love to your friends. But in the end, trust God with the results of those efforts. Proverbs 16:9 says,

> *"A man's heart deviseth his way: but the LORD directeth his steps."*

This gives us a solid view of the direction God is leading us by asking for our complete surrender to Him.

God blessed us with free will and wants us to make decisions. He also wants us to surrender the control of our situations and the results of what happens in our lives to Him. God wants us to live our lives, but also be willing to lay our plans aside in order to let Him guide us when He needs to.

Surrender is about many different things that we must give to God to build and maintain the bridge of communication with Him. We must give our time, we must give our obedience, and we must give ourselves.

We need to read the Bible on a regular basis. This is how we learn more about what God wants from us and for us. Reading the Bible gives us the foundational knowledge that we need to be ready to face what the world will throw at us. When the devil attacks us, the Bible is our primary weapon against him. Quoting Scripture in times of trouble or strife—or even just whispering Jesus' name—will cause the demons to scatter.

One of the main reasons that I have left it until now to discuss the value of the Bible to Christians is because we've been using great men of faith as examples. It is clear that Jesus and David knew the law that would become the Old Testament of the Bible, and Moses received this law directly from God, but the entirety of the Bible and its knowledge and inspiration was not there for them to use.

Let me be clear, the Bible is vital to our relationship with God. The Bible is God's Word and we need to make sure we know His Word to be obedient. This part falls under surrender because we must know what we are led by and how we are to obey in order to truly surrender to God.

As we have in previous chapters, we will look at the lives of Moses, David, and Jesus to see how they surrendered themselves to God's will for their lives.

How Moses Surrendered

We will focus on Moses first. Moses was a wonderful example of surrendering to God's will. Think about it: would you want to wander around in the desert for 40 years with a group of people that complain and fight the entire time? I would not want to do that. However, this is exactly what Moses did. We can look at Hebrews 11:23-29 for a summary of these things that Moses did in the name of God and not himself. He surrendered to God.

Moses showed several times that he was not the ruler of his life. He was born into a bad situation, but God worked it out for him. Moses grew and became closer to the Lord and ultimately was chosen to lead the Israelites out of bondage. Now this is not to say that Moses was obedient right away. Moses tried to make excuses for why he couldn't do what God had called him to do. These five excuses are reflected in the narrative as found in Exodus 3 and 4.

His excuses begin with himself as he asks God about his credentials (Exodus 3:11). He basically asks, in his conversation with God, why should Pharaoh listen to me? What sort of authority would I have that would cause Pharaoh to even listen to me?

His second excuse is found in verse 13 of the same chapter. Here Moses asks: By whose authority would I be approaching Pharaoh? What is the name of this God that has sent me?

Moses' next objection to God's calling is found in Exodus 4:1. Here he insists they will not believe him, and therefore they will not listen to what he has to say.

Moses continues to raise objections in verse 10 of this chapter, saying that he is not a gifted speaker, that he is not eloquent, and that in fact he is of *"slow of speech and of a slow tongue."*

Finally, in Exodus 4:13 Moses pleads, *"Oh my Lord, send, I pray thee, by the hand of him whom thou wilt send."* Here, in essence, Moses is basically saying please send somebody else.

One excuse after another was offered by Moses to God as to why he should not be the one to go to Pharaoh. But God would not take no for an answer, and for each excuse offered, God revealed Himself even further to Moses.

These revelations include first His promise to be with Moses as seen in Exodus 3:12. In Exodus 3:14, God reveals His name by sharing with Moses that He is *"I AM THAT I AM."* revealing His name. God is powerfully stating and affirming to Moses that He is. He is everything we need or require. For the believer, a blank space follows this affirmation of He is and we can fill in the blank.

To answer the three remaining objections raised by Moses, God reveals and verifies His power as Creator. By turning the rod into a serpent and back again and making Moses' hand leprous, God reveals His power. (Exodus 4:2-4) Finally, God says to Moses that he and his brother, Aaron, will go to Pharaoh's court and that God will use them as His spokespersons. (Exodus 4:14-16)

How powerful it is to realize that the very God who spoke the world into existence and that the very Word that became flesh (John 1:14), would now speak through Moses and demand of an earthy ruler to *"Let my people go"* (Exodus 5:1).

Additionally, God commands Moses to *"take this rod in thine hand"* (Exodus 4:17). It is important not to miss the significance of the rod. The rod of Moses was a mere shepherd's crook made out of wood, but in the hand of a committed servant of God it became a powerful instrument of service and reflection of surrender.

Surrender because as a tool to tend the sheep, we are reminded that a shepherd is willing to surrender their life for the flock (John 10:11). Also, this rod belonging to Moses had the ability—because of God's power—to transform a surrendered object or life. This transformation was witnessed when the rod became a serpent and then turned back into a rod again.

Additionally, the rod no longer belonged to Moses, but in Exodus 4:20 is referred to as "the rod of God." Also, when the rod touched the waters of Egypt (Exodus 7:19), the water was turned to blood. Perhaps, without being too much of a stretch, a correlation can be made between the power of the cross of Christ and this rod. Both the rod and the cross are powerful (1 Corinthians 1:18), reflective of a surrendered life (Luke 9:23), and have the ability to transform (Galatians 6:14).

And so Moses, with the rod of God in hand, surrendered his self-doubt and fear to God and went to see the Pharaoh. Moses surrendered his fears and was willing to go back several times to the Pharaoh, commanding him to let God's people go (Exodus 9-10). This example of surrender is both one of faith in God's plan and surrender of self.

Eventually God softened the Pharaoh's heart, and he allowed Moses to take the Israelites. This was nowhere close to the end, though. Moses started to take the Israelites out of Egypt, but the Pharaoh changed his mind and chased after them. Moses and his people arrived at the Red Sea with nowhere to go. Moses had a choice, and instead of trying to fix the situation himself he turned to God. Moses surrendered his thoughts and himself to God and God started to work. God protected the people from the Egyptians and then spoke to Moses saying:

> *Wherefore criest thou unto me? speak unto the children of Israel, that they go forward: But lift thou up thy rod, and stretch out thine hand over the sea, and divide it: and the children of Israel shall go on dry ground through the midst of the sea.* (Exodus 14:15-16)

Let's take a step back here. God told Moses to take the rod he was holding and stretch it out over the Red Sea, which would divide. This was a huge moment for Moses and for the Israelites.

What would Moses have looked like if he had stretched out his rod and nothing happened? The Israelites would have been captured and Moses would have more than likely been killed, or at best been ridiculed for the rest of his life for being so foolish to think that he could have been the one that would lead the people of God out of bondage.

But God is faithful. He kept His word, and as Moses stretched out his rod over the sea, it parted, and the Israelites were able to walk across as if they were on dry land. God honored the surrender of Moses' will and doubts by showing everyone that He was the One in control and the One working through Moses.

As we discussed earlier, the Israelites were still complaining and coming to Moses with everything that was going wrong. What did Moses do? He took it all to God. He surrendered himself and his leadership to God's will. Moses led these people for 40 years in the wilderness. He watched God honor this perseverance by supplying manna for them to eat, water from a rock, and clothing that did not wear or tear for 40 years in the wilderness.

Eventually Moses and the Israelites came upon the Promised Land. Moses knew he could not go in, but God graced him by letting him see the Promise Land. I think most people would have just thrown their hands up in frustration and walked away. Not Moses. Moses knew that he would not be allowed to lead the people into the Promised Land, so he surrendered himself to God's plan and chose his successor, Joshua, to lead. Moses helped Joshua to prepare for this calling, rather than working against him as many would have done in this situation.

How David Surrendered

As with Moses, David came from humble beginnings. We first learn about David as a shepherd boy. We learn that he fellowshipped with and sought God regularly. This was the foundation of David's anointing: his surrender to and seeking of God.

As a boy, David was anointed as king. This may have gone to many people's heads, but it did not go to David's head at all. He continued as a shepherd as if nothing had really happened.

David realized that God was in control and that his rise to fulfilling his anointing as king would come when God planned. This showed extreme trust and surrender to God's will. That is not to say he was not happy or that he didn't feel blessed, but he did not become someone who thought of himself as being overly important.

David was tending the flock when his father sent him to the battlefield to take supplies to his brothers. This unknowingly became a turning point for David. As David arrived where his brothers were fighting, he heard a Philistine named Goliath. Goliath was beating his chest and challenging the army of God, and they were just taking it. Goliath even started to mock God. This did not sit well with David and he went to Saul to ask for permission to challenge Goliath.

To set the scene here, Goliath was the Philistine champion and was said to be over nine feet tall. Goliath had been trained since an early age to be a warrior and had become the champion of the Philistines due to his amazing feats and his great victories. David, on the other hand, was a shepherd boy that just came to bring his brothers supplies.

What a mismatch! David said that he was not afraid. He spoke of how he had killed a bear as well as a lion and that this Philistine would be no different. Eventually, he was able to convince the king and went to face Goliath. David faced the giant with five stones and a sling. No armor, no sword, no protection—at least no outward protection. Goliath taunted David and continued to blaspheme God.

David did not go into this battle for himself. David faced Goliath for God. He was willing to surrender himself and put his life on the line to show the power of God. God could have used anyone to do this, but David was willing to surrender himself and be obedient to God. A huge part of surrender is the willingness to be obedient in any condition or circumstance.

As we know, David faced Goliath and defeated him. This victory was assured because David was on the side of God and not trying to work for himself, by his own power, or for his own glory. As you can imagine, this victory made David famous and popular. This was a huge moment where David would show his true colors.

Not that David was perfect in his life, but he was a man who did not, for the most part, let his fame and high stature with others change him as a person. David became a great warrior and leader of men in battle. This made him even more famous.

The fame and attention that David was receiving started to bother King Saul and make him jealous of David. Eventually, Saul would try to kill David. Now most of us would probably take an opportunity to get rid of someone that was trying to kill us, but David did not because he had such deep respect for God's chosen king. He surrendered his own wellbeing for this respect. In fact, David had two separate opportunities to kill King Saul. David did let King Saul know that he had those chances, but did not take them, hoping that this fact would influence Saul's thoughts about him.

Saul, knowing that David was the anointed king, asked David for mercy for him and his family. It would have been fairly easy for David to have let his own emotions and free will get in the way, but David surrendered himself. He let God move through him. He gave mercy and grace to Saul and his family.

One additional powerful insight into David's actions in surrendering to God is recorded for us in Psalm 51. This Psalm is the response of David to that event in his life when God's prophet, Nathan, confronted him about his sinful relationship with Bathsheba. These words of surrender flow from David's broken heart as he realizes that he has grieved God.

In verses 1-11 of this psalm we see the formula for a surrendering prayer. It is important to note, however, that the *"effectual fervent prayer of a righteous man"* (James 5:16) is not uttered by following a liturgical outline. A prayer of surrender must emanate from the heart. It must flow. It must be real and not uttered by rote.

From the depths of David's being we see that he calls upon God. A prayer of surrender in order to obtain God's victory must be directed to God. David cries out, *"Have mercy upon me, O God"* (Psalm 51:1) It is a desperate prayer, and without God's redeeming answer, David is lost. We are lost. David cries out, *"Against Thee, Thee only have I sinned"* (51:4), recognizing that only from God could he obtain lovingkindness and mercy.

Secondly, in this prayer of surrender from David we hear his confession. David states, *"For I acknowledge my transgressions and my sin is ever before me"* (Psalm 51:3). We can safely declare that in this verse, David is overwrought. He feels and senses the devastating effects of sin and his subsequent separation from God because of it.

The third aspect of a David's prayer of surrender is his cry to be purged. He desires to be clean and made as white as snow

(Psalm 51:7). He surrenders his sin-stained heart to the cleansing flow of God's mercy and grace.

In Jeremiah 17:9 we are reminded, "The heart is deceitful above all things, and desperately wicked: who can know it?" David's prayer of surrender and handing it all over to God includes being keenly aware of how sick his heart is and how it can betray his relationship with God. And so, David pleads with God for a repairing of his broken bones (51:8) and the creation of a clean heart (51:10).

Finally, because of his calling out to God and God's cleansing, David, in his surrendering prayer, asks that God not take His Holy Spirit from him. Additionally, he asks for restoration and a return of God's joy. (Psalm 51:12)

David faced many different challenges in his life where he could have made the decision to try to fix things by his own power. Instead, he surrendered himself and sought God's will for his life.

.

How Jesus Surrendered

Jesus spoke about surrendering to God on a regular basis. Just as we read in Matthew 16:24-25:

> *Then said Jesus unto his disciples, If any man will come after me, let him deny himself, and take up his cross, and follow me. For whosoever will save his life shall lose it: and whosoever will lose his life for my sake shall find it.*

That is a powerful statement. If we want to follow Jesus, and in turn follow God, we must deny ourselves. In other words, we must surrender ourselves and take up our burdens to go with Him. We must not only seek Him; we must be willing to let go of what we want to have and let God be in control.

Think about it this way: We only have two hands. We can try to sort things and rearrange them, but there is only so much we can lift with our hands. If we want a closer relationship with God, we need to have both hands free to grab on to Him and let Him lead us.

This was not the only time Jesus spoke about surrender, though. When we read Luke 14:11 we see this concept again: *"For whosoever exalteth himself shall be abased; and he that humbleth himself shall be exalted."* We should make sure we are lifting up the right things in our lives; the things that are in God's will for us. This can be hard with all the temptations of the world and all the people around us seemingly gaining from being worldly.

We need to realize where we are building our treasures. Jesus tells us in Matthew 6:19-21:

> *Lay not up for yourselves treasures upon earth, where moth and rust doth corrupt, and where thieves break through and steal: But lay up for yourselves treasures in heaven, where neither moth nor rust doth corrupt, and where thieves do not break through nor steal: For where your treasure is, there will your heart be also.*

This is a verse we should have highlighted, circled, and underlined in our Bibles. It is a scripture that I lean on daily when the world is tempting my family and me. Where do you want your treasures to be: on earth or in heaven?

Jesus not only taught about surrender but also practiced it for us to see as an example. As a child, He subjected Himself to being born in a way that was not fitting for His true stature and what He deserved. He surrendered His comfort and status with a humble beginning. There is no doubt that God planned this.

As Jesus grew up, He chose to surrender to His Heavenly Father by being baptized. This was an outward way of showing us that He was submitting and surrendering His will to God's will. There is probably no better scripture to see what Jesus thought about surrender than John 5:30:

> *"I can of mine own self do nothing: as I hear, I judge: and my judgment is just; because I seek not mine own will, but the will of the Father which hath sent me."*

This is the Son of God, yet throughout His life, He did the Father's will, not His own. He even refused to use His power and stood with God for His own deliverance as shown in the Garden of Gethsemane. He prayed three separate times for the cup to pass, but the key to this prayer was that He asked that it all be God's will and not His own. God already knew the will of Jesus as a human was to have this pain and suffering pass Him over if there was any other way to pay the debt for our sins and offer salvation for mankind. Jesus knew that His will was nowhere near as important as God's will. God could see the big picture. His intentions were for the entire world to have access to Him. The most convicting fact was that with His dying breath, Jesus surrendered His spirit to the Father. We see in Matthew 27:50 the final moments of Jesus' life where it says: *"Jesus, when he had cried again with a loud voice, yielded up the ghost."* Jesus surrendered Himself and remained obedient even unto death.

CONCLUSION

We should be able and willing to surrender ourselves to God. God has a plan in place that we need to follow, but He will not force it on us. God wanted to show us examples in the Bible of how we are to surrender ourselves, and the examples of Moses, David, and Jesus are just a few that we can see in His Word.

BRINGING IT
All Together

Simply following this recipe and doing nothing else will not guarantee you a great relationship with God. This may come as a shock. You read this book about the recipe for a closer relationship with God, but it did not give the whole recipe! That is like getting a cookbook from the store and part of each recipe is blacked out!

As I mentioned before, these four ingredients are the main ingredients. I said there are other spices and flavorings that we have to add in to make it great. Every great chef puts their own unique twist on a dish by adding various seasonings. That is how we need to look at our relationship with God. Some of these spices and flavorings are: reading God's Word, fasting, fellowship with other Christians, and other additives as God leads you. There is a wide assortment of spices that we need to add to this recipe, and they will change as we learn and grow as Christians. However, the main ingredients of our recipe for a closer relationship with God are constant and required.

The relationship we have with God is a reflection of many things. It reflects our mind, heart, and spirit. This vital relationship mirrors us. It is personal and it is sacred. The amazing thing is that the process of building your relationship with God can be simple and difficult at the same time. The concepts are basically simple: Prayer, Praise, Perseverance, and Surrender. However, putting these four characteristics into real-life practice can often be very difficult for the modern-day Christian.

God has provided many examples in the Bible to reinforce this recipe for a closer relationship with Him. Just as we discussed earlier, some of the strongest examples we find in the Bible are Moses, David, and Jesus Christ.

If these examples of close relationships with God are to be our examples, then we need to realize that we are not asked to be perfect. With the exception of Jesus, every man and woman in the Bible had sin in his or her life. These mighty men and women of God did some things that would make you second-guess their credibility. Thankfully, God does not look for perfect people to use—He looks for willing people. Each man and woman set as an example in Scripture sinned against God, with the exception of Jesus. This is a characteristic that they all shared. However, they also shared the fact that they were willing to seek after God and His will.

What do we need to do? We must take the time to learn from God. We have to focus on His will; we have to do the work. As I stated earlier, God is the constant and we are the variable. God wants us to be closer to Him, but He will not change for us. We have to change for Him.

I have heard it said before by some people that God is on their side. I don't see this as true. God does not choose sides. God does not choose sides in an agreement. He does not choose sides in your problems. God does not choose sides in your church, and He does not choose sides in relationships. We choose the side we will stand on, and God is either already there or not. Don't think God will change for you. You have to change for Him and everyone you reach. You have to choose His side.

If you truly have a desire to be closer to God, you can get there. It will be difficult at some points. It will be uncomfortable for many. Remember this: we are warriors for God, and a warrior does not fight against the people in his army. The enemy does not fight us as hard when we are doing the worldly things that he wants us to do. It is when we choose to be in the Army of God and fight against the enemy that he starts to fight back.

If you remember nothing else from this book, I want you to be able to put this simple fact very close to your heart: God loves you and cares for you, but you determine the distance between yourself and God. God does not change. We are the ones who change and move. God doesn't take His eyes off you; you take your eyes off Him. So keep your eye on the prize—the reward is great! As stated in Isaiah 40:31:

> *"But they that wait upon the Lord shall renew their strength; they shall mount up with wings as eagles; they shall run, and not be weary; and they shall walk, and not faint."*

In summary, each person can accept Jesus Christ as their Savior, become a Christian, and develop an open line of communication with God. Using this recipe for a closer relationship with God, each Christian can nurture and cultivate their own individualized relationship with their Heavenly Father using prayer, giving praise to God, perseverance, and the surrender of self as the foundational ingredients. Walking hand-in-hand with God is easy when we let Him be in control. However, when we decide that we know what is best and start making decisions without consulting Him, we are headed for failure.

GREAT MEN AND WOMEN
of the Bible

Abigail: When Abigail's husband refused to treat David and his men with hospitality, he put the lives of his whole household at risk. That's when Abigail took charge, sending offerings of food and a message of peace. Ultimately, Abigail's wisdom brought peace and saved the lives of those around her. (Read Abigail's story in 1 Samuel 25)

Abraham: Abraham was married to Sarah, and is often thought of as the Father of all Jewish people. He was a man of great faith. God asked him to leave his home and travel hundreds of miles away to a new home. When he started the journey, he didn't know where he was going, but he trusted God to lead him. (Read Abraham's story in Genesis 12-25)

Achsah: Achsah stepped out in faith and claimed additional blessing for her family because she was bold enough to ask for more. Just like our heavenly Father is ready and willing to bless us, we must also go to Him with this same faith. (Read Achsah's story in Joshua 15)

Anna: Anna appears in just a few verses of Scripture, but it's during a pivotal moment: when Jesus' parents present Him at the temple. After Mary and Joseph arrive, they find Anna at her usual spot in the temple, fasting and praying. When she meets them, she gives thanks to God for the child in their arms—because He will set Jerusalem free. (Read Anna's story in Luke 2:36-38)

Barnabas: Barnabas played a large role in the establishment of new churches in the Greek and Hebrew world of his day. Barnabas was the man who took Paul under his wing when no one else wanted to trust him. Barnabas trained Paul in the ministry and accompanied him on his early missionary travels. (Read Barnabas' story in Acts 15)

Daniel: Daniel came from a very important family in Jerusalem. When the king of Babylon defeated his country, he was taken captive along with some of his friends. They were treated very well in this foreign country; they were given a university education and offered jobs in the royal court. But some of the customs of the Babylonian people were against Daniel's beliefs. He did not want to stop worshipping the one true God, so he stuck to his principles even though it could have cost him his job, or even his life! He was rewarded with a top job in the government. (Read Daniel's story in Daniel 6)

David: David started life as a shepherd boy. He quickly grew into a brave teenager who protected his flock from mountain lions. His great skill with a catapult helped him defeat a giant called Goliath even when all the King's soldiers were too scared to fight. Multiple times in the Bible, David is recognized as a man who followed God and was sensitive to the leadership of God in his life. (Read David's story in 1 Samuel)

Deborah: When Israel was in the middle of crisis, Deborah stepped in to play a pivotal leadership role. She served as a judge for the people and provided crucial guidance for another leader from Israel—Barak—to go into a battle that would free Israel from its oppressors. (Read Deborah's story in Judges 4-5)

Elijah: Elijah was a prophet with a rugged look and a blunt way of speaking. He was never afraid to tell even kings and queens when he felt they were behaving badly! Sometimes this got him into trouble, but he always wanted to tell the truth. (Read Elijah's story in 1 Kings 17 – 2 Kings 2)

Elisha: Elisha became a prophet through Elijah, who asked him to become part of his "prophetic team." A prophet is someone who God has asked to let people know what He is going to do in the future. (Read Elisha's story in 2 Kings 1-13)

Enoch: Enoch was a loyal follower of God. He told the truth despite opposition and ridicule. Enoch holds a rare distinction in the Bible: He did not die. Instead, God "took him away."

Scripture does not reveal much about this remarkable man. (Read Enoch's story in Genesis 5)

Esther: Esther was a girl who God used to help His people in a very special way. She was a Jew, living a very long way from home, in a country where the Jews were looked at with suspicion. (Read Esther's story in the book of Esther)

Hannah: Although Hannah went years without bearing a child, she continued to pray in faith for God to provide her with a child. Eventually, He did: Samuel. Hannah dedicated her son to the Lord, and he grew up to be a wise and respected judge for the nation of Israel. (Read Hannah's story in 1 Samuel 1)

Isaiah: Isaiah is widely regarded as one of the greatest prophets of the Bible. He lived in Jerusalem and the prophecies God gave him were directed toward Israel, Judah, and other nations. Jewish tradition says he was of royal descent, and he may have been a cousin to King Uzziah. This may have given him access to the kings of Judah in Jerusalem. (Read Isaiah's story in the book of Isaiah)

Jeremiah: God called Jeremiah when he was still a youth. In fact, God had already set Jeremiah apart for the office of a prophet before he was even born, to take God's words to all Israel and to the nations. God gave Jeremiah the overview of his prophetic ministry. This meant that God had appointed

Jeremiah to proclaim the destruction and rebuilding of nations that would eventually lead to the Kingdom of God. (Read Jeremiah's story in the book of Jeremiah)

Jesus: Jesus came to us for a reason: to take our sin upon Himself in order that we could be blameless in God's eyes. And if that isn't enough, He was completely sinless! He did not commit one single sin ever. Now He is definitely someone inspiring! Jesus experienced all the temptations we do. He was tempted in every way and He came out a champion! He laid down His life for us, and that, my friends, is the greatest act of love anyone can do. (Read Jesus' story in the books of Matthew, Mark, Luke, and John)

Job: Satan was talking with God one day when he said that no one completely obeyed God and worshiped Him. God said that He knew a man who was just and upright in his life. God gave Satan rule over Job's circumstances, causing him to lose all his wealth. Job still would not speak evil against God. He even acknowledged that God was the one who was testing him and he would continue to worship the Lord. (Read Job's story in the book of Job)

John the Baptist: John the Baptist lived at the same time as Jesus. Their mothers (Elizabeth and Mary) were related and so they probably saw each other from time to time as they were growing up. God gave John a special role: letting everyone know that Jesus was coming soon. (Read John the Baptist's story in Luke 3)

Joseph (earthly father of Jesus): Joseph was the earthly father of Jesus; the man entrusted with raising the Son of God. Joseph was also a carpenter or skilled craftsman. He obeyed God in the face of severe humiliation. He did the right thing before God, in the right manner. Joseph was a man of strong conviction who lived out his beliefs in his actions. He was described in the Bible as a righteous man. Even when personally wronged, he had the quality of being sensitive to someone else's shame. He responded to God in obedience and he practiced self-control. Joseph is a wonderful biblical example of integrity and godly character. (Read Joseph's story in Luke 1-2)

Joseph (Old Testament): The story of Joseph is an amazing story because it reveals how God—in His foreknowledge—planned far in advance, knowing that the Jews wouldn't survive in Canaan because of the coming famine and other circumstances, but needed to be brought down into Egypt where they would not only survive but multiply exceedingly. God ordained the situation with Joseph to preserve His people and fulfill His promises to Abraham. (Read Joseph's story in Genesis 41-50)

Joshua: Joshua was an obedient follower. He was also known as a strong leader of Israel as it was under his leadership that they conquered the land that God had given. (Read Joshua's story in the book of Joshua)

Mary Magdalene: Mary Magdalene was delivered from a life of demonic oppression and experienced the resurrected power of Christ. Thus, she was one of the first to announce the risen Christ. (Read Mary Magdalene's story in Matthew 27-28:1; Mark 15-16; Luke 8 and 24; John 19-20)

Mary (mother of Jesus): Mary was just a young girl when an angel appeared to her and told her she would bring the Messiah—Jesus—into the world. Yet she responded to this daunting task by praising God. Then she went about the task of raising Him, even when it meant fleeing to Egypt to protect Him. Mary surrendered her life and her reputation to the purposes of God. Her submission shows us that when we consecrate our life to the Lord, He can do amazing things.

(Read Mary's story in Luke 1:26-56)

Moses: When he was three months old, Moses was put into a waterproof basket on the Nile River so that he would not be harmed. Moses was a Jew, and the king of Egypt wanted to stop the Jewish nation from growing too large and powerful, so he ordered all the Jewish baby boys to be killed! God kept Moses safe, and even arranged for the king's daughter to find Moses on the river and bring him up as her own child. (Read Moses' story in Exodus 2-13)

Noah: Noah really wanted to live God's way, so God told him to build an ark that could contain all the different kinds of animals. Noah, his wife, their three sons, and their sons' wives built the boat and gathered the animals inside it. Once the door was closed God sent a heavy rain that covered everything with water for a long time. At last the rain stopped, and after waiting a while Noah sent out a raven and then a dove to see if they could find land. Noah and his family were safe and well—kept safe by God. Then God promised that he would not flood the whole world again, so people need not be afraid every time it rained. Every time you see a rainbow in the sky, you are looking at the sign God gave Noah to remind him of this promise. (Read Noah's story in Genesis 6-9)

Paul: Paul was a great man of the New Testament. We first see this man when his name was Saul of Tarsus. Before his salvation, he was convinced that Jesus and Christianity were plots to destroy the Hebrew God of the Old Testament. However, Jesus revealed Himself to Saul, who then accepted the Lord as his personal Savior. Instead of persecuting the Church, Saul changed his name to Paul and began to preach and establish new churches throughout the known world. (Read Paul's story in the book of Acts)

Peter: Peter was one of the first people to become a friend of Jesus. He was a fisherman on the Sea of Galilee when he met Jesus. He was impetuous—which means sometimes he rushed into things and said things before thinking about them! (Read Peter's story in John 1 and 18; Acts 2-3)

Ruth: Even though Ruth wasn't an Israelite, she remained loyal to her Israelite mother-in-law, Naomi. She followed Naomi back to her homeland and married Boaz, the next-of-kin, to continue the family line, provide for Naomi, and ultimately become an ancestor of Jesus. (Read Ruth's story in Ruth 1-4)

Samuel: His mother, Hannah, did not think she would be able to have children and so it was a great answer to her prayers when Samuel arrived! She was so thankful to God that she wanted Samuel to have the task of serving in the temple. It was here that God called Samuel to be a leader of his people. He wasn't very old when he heard God speak to him for the first time, and God asked him to do something that was very difficult: tell the priest Eli that something terrible was going to happen to him and his family. (Read Samuel's story in 1 Samuel 9-10)

Sarah: Sarah demonstrated faith and obedience while believing God's promises. She left her comfortable and familiar surroundings to launch her journey with God. (Read Sarah's story in Genesis 12-25)

Shadrach, Meshach, and Abednego: These three men refused to worship the golden idol set up by King Nebuchadnezzar, even though they knew they would be thrown into a blazing hot furnace. The furnace was so hot that the guards that threw them in it died! They were faithful to God, so He delivered them from the furnace. (Read their story in Daniel 3)

Tabitha: Not only did Tabitha inspire others by serving the poor and widows around her, the story of Peter raising her from the dead inspired many to follow Jesus in the early days of the church. (Read Tabitha's story in Acts 9:36-43)

www.ingramcontent.com/pod-product-compliance
Lightning Source LLC
Chambersburg PA
CBHW020618300426
44113CB00007B/689